Victor Serge :
revolution in danger

revolution in danger
Victor Serge
writings from Russia 1919/1920

During the civil war
The endangered city
The anarchists and the experience of the Russian revolution

Translated from the French by Ian Birchall

Victor Serge: Revolution in danger
  During the civil war
  The endangered city
  The anarchists and the experience of the Russian revolution
First published 1997 by
REDWORDS
1 Bloomsbury Street, London WC1B 3QE

Printed with permission from the Victor Serge Foundation
Translation © Ian Birchall

ISBN: 1 872208 08 8

Design and production: Roger Huddle & Rob Hoveman
Set in 9/12pt Adobe Janson
Imagesetting by East End Offset Ltd, London E3
Printed by BPC Wheatons Ltd., Exeter, England

Contents

REDWORDS operates as a publishing
co-operative producing books,
mainly fictional, cultural and historical,
from a socialist perspective.
We are linked to BOOKMARKS.

REDWORDS would like to thank
the following people for helping
to publish this book:
Richard Greeman from the *Victor Serge Foundation*
Sofie Mason
Mac McKenna
Mary Phillips

INTRODUCTION: **Victor Serge** was witness to, and participant in, many of the great political upheavals of the first half of this century. Born in Brussels of Russian revolutionary parents in 1890, he moved as a young man to Paris where he became active in the anarchist movement. Jailed from 1913 to 1917 after defending the anarchist bank robbers of the Bonnot Gang, he participated in the failed syndicalist insurrection of 1917 in Barcelona before going to revolutionary Russia. As a Comintern journalist he observed the defeat of the German revolution in 1923, returned to Russia where he supported the Left Opposition, was sent into internal exile in the remote town of Orenburg, then expelled from the USSR. Back in the West he continued his fight for authentic socialism, helping to expose the counter-revolutionary role of Stalinism in the Spanish civil war. When the Nazis occupied France he took refuge in Mexico, where he died in 1947. The defeats and triumphs of the period are described in his novels, in his magnificent *Memoirs of a Revolutionary* and his many political writings. In his later years Serge became one of the outstanding critics of Stalinism, but his critique was always rooted in the traditions of the early years of the Russian Revolution.

Serge arrived in Russia in February 1919 and in May he decided to become a member of the Communist Party. To Serge's comrades in the anarchist movement this must have seemed a highly questionable step; but his writings of the next few years, notably the pamphlets published here, provide a powerful justification for his decision. While throwing himself into the frenetic activity required by the period, Serge maintained and developed his political contacts in France, and over the next few years wrote a large number of articles explaining and defending the Russian Revolution for a range of journals of the French left.

In 1921 he published two short pamphlets, *During the civil war* and *The anarchists and the experience of the Russian revolution* in the series edited by Marcel Martinet, *Les Cahiers du travail* (Labour Notebooks).[1] The previous year he had written a series of articles in the syndicalist journal *La Vie ouvrière* entitled *The endangered city*. An extended version was published in pamphlet form in 1924.[2] These three pamphlets together form a unity; there is much overlap of theme and content, and they provide a unique source of documentation.[3] Apart from very short extracts[4], none of Serge's writing from this period has been available in English.[5]

There is an important difference between the three texts translated here and Serge's later works. In the later texts, even when he was recounting the early years of the revolution, he was writing under the shadow of Stalinism. He was aware of the outcome of the revolution, and often seemed to be consciously looking for causes in the earliest years which could help to explain how the monstrosity of Stalinism came about.[6]

There is no such hindsight present in these pamphlets. They have the freshness of immediacy and, even more, the power of revolutionary enthusiasm. That is not to say that they are naïve or that they lack critical judgement; on the contrary. But they convey a vivid sense of what it was actually like to experience the first years of the revolution. In 1944 Serge wrote: 'There is nobody left who knows what the Russian revolution was really like, what the Bolsheviks were really like—and men judge without knowing, with bitterness and basic rigidity'.[7] But perhaps if anything can recreate that historical reality, it is Serge's vivid and concrete prose.

Serge's strategy in writing the pamphlets must be seen in the context of the hopes for a rapid spread of the revolution, and in particular of the situation of the French left in 1921. The French Communist Party had been formed in 1920 when the majority of the Socialist Party voted to affiliate to the Communist International. But the winning of the main working-class party to the cause of the October revolution brought with it many problems—not least the fact that the party had brought with it a large number of careerists and opportunists who were going along with the popularity of the revolution but had not abandoned their old habits. (A typical example was the odious Marcel Cachin, who had been a virulent nationalist during the course of World War I and went on to be a pillar of French Stalinism.)

Yet many of the best militants in France had never been members of the Socialist Party. They had been anarchists, or, in many cases, the political cousins of anarchism, revolutionary syndicalists. People like Rosmer, Monatte and Martinet had been at the forefront of opposition to the war in 1914 and had supported the October revolution at the very outset when most of the Socialist Party were still keeping their distance.

Potentially such militants had a key role to play in building a genuine revolutionary communist party in France. Trotsky recounts a meeting with Lenin when the latter said to him: 'Could we not advise the French communists to drive out those corrupt parliamentarians Cachin and Frossard and replace them with the [syndicalist] *Vie ouvrière group?*' [8] This strategy in turn must be placed in the context of the Bolshevik efforts to win syndicalists and anarchists to the cause of the Communist International— especially through the founding of the Red International of Labour Unions. [9]

The person directly responsible for publishing two of the three pamphlets was Marcel Martinet (1887-1944), a significant figure on the French left around 1920. He had been associated with the small group of revolutionary syndicalists who had opposed the war from the first day in 1914; he had known Trotsky during his time in Paris—Trotsky wrote that 'his whole person breathed simplicity, intelligence, nobility of soul'. [10] He was an

accomplished poet; his anti-war poems *Les temps maudits*
(Accursed Times) were banned in France during the war but
circulated clandestinely; with the assistance of Marguerite Rosmer
copies were typed on thin paper and enclosed in letters sent to
soldiers at the front. He was also a gifted dramatist[11] and novelist.[12]
He was a founder member of the French Communist Party and in
1921 became editor of the cultural page in the party's daily paper,
L'Humanité. He was an advocate of the idea of 'proletarian
culture'—though he used the term somewhat differently to the
way in which it was used in the contemporary debates in Russia,
seeing it rather in terms of a struggle to raise the cultural level of
the proletariat. To this end he launched the *Cahiers du travail*, a
series of fortnightly pamphlets, in 1921. Only twelve issues
appeared, but as well as Serge's two pamphlets Martinet published
Rosa Luxemburg's *Letters from Prison*, and texts by the former
French syndicalists Rosmer and Monatte and the Bolsheviks
Shlyapnikov and Lozovsky. Martinet abandoned active politics
from 1924 for health reasons, but he remained close to the anti-
Stalinist left and wrote a pamphlet in defence of Serge at the time
of the campaign to release him from exile in Russia.[13]

The Russia in which Serge found himself in 1919 faced
appalling dangers. In 1917, amid the horrors of trench warfare,
the October Revolution had given millions of soldiers and
working people the hope of a real alternative. Over the next three
or four years world revolution seemed like a very real short-term
possibility; it is only in the context of that possibility that we can
understand why so many from different traditions were prepared
to stand and fight alongside the Bolsheviks.

For that very reason the October revolution inspired fear
and fury among the ruling classes of the West. On the day *before*
the Armistice in 1918 Winston Churchill told the war cabinet it
might be necessary to rebuild the German army to fight against
Bolshevism. Two weeks later he told a meeting:

> Civilisation is being completely extinguished over gigantic
> areas, while Bolsheviks hop and caper like troops of
> ferocious baboons amid the ruins of cities and the corpses of
> their victims.[14]

As a clear-sighted adversary of the working class, Churchill knew who his real enemies were. (He also, of course, knew his real friends; it was the same Churchill who, in 1944, sat down with Stalin to carve up Eastern Europe on a half sheet of paper.[15])

The reactionary Russian generals who were waging war against the Bolshevik regime received massive assistance from the capitalist world. Fourteen nations—including Britain, France, the USA, Canada, Czechoslovakia and Japan—sent military forces totalling many tens of thousands of men to assist in the onslaught against the newly established workers' state.

Knowing that their whole future was at stake, the defenders of the old order fought with utter ruthlessness. Even the minimal conventions of military decency that had been observed in the First World War were abandoned. A correspondent of the *Manchester Guardian* reported on the behaviour of the counter-revolutionary White armies in 1919:

It was difficult to know what was done with prisoners...
When questioned on the subject, the White officers always said: 'Oh, we kill all of them that are Communists'. Jews and commissaries stood no chance, of course, but it was somewhat difficult to ascertain which of the others were Communists. The system generally followed was this. From among the prisoners a man who 'looked like a Bolshevik' was led aside, accused with great violence of being a notorious Communist, but afterwards promised that his life would be spared if he gave the names of all those among his companions whom he knew to belong to the Bolshevik Party. This ingenious scheme, which was tried on more than one victim in each party of prisoners, generally resulted in a number of Red soldiers being executed.[16]

The US Commander in Siberia in 1919, General William S Graves, testified that 'I am well on the side of safety when I say that the anti-Bolsheviks killed one hundred people in Eastern Siberia, to every one killed by the Bolsheviks'.[17]

In this situation Serge had no doubts about which side he was on. The revolution was engaged in a war to the death with its bitterest enemies, and the whole future of the world seemed to depend on the outcome of that war. Only by grasping the profound international significance of the events in Russia can we understand how a former anarchist was able to accept Bolshevik terror. Whatever his reservations about Bolshevik theory and practice, Serge aligned himself unconditionally with the Bolshevik side. As he wrote many years later: 'the most outraged observations of the anti-Bolshevik intellectuals only revealed to me how necessary Bolshevism was'.[18]

These pamphlets are a striking testimony to Serge's commitment. What shines through every line of the text is Serge's enthusiasm for the revolution, its achievements, its leaders and its ideals.

In particular he stresses the moral superiority of the Bolsheviks. Nowadays morality is all too often nothing but a cliché for politicians who lack any concrete policies. Serge's concept of morality is very different; he sees it as a corrective to a marxism which, in the epoch of the Second International, had often excluded morality in favour of a mechanical economic determinism.

Serge insists that it is the 'moral force' of the proletariat which underpins its historical superiority and guarantees its victory. His account of the enormous sacrifices made by the inhabitants of Petrograd, of the mass mobilisation made in the defence of the city, gives a striking account of how material and moral factors complement and reinforce each other.

At the same time he recognises the grim necessities of revolutionary defence. In particular he is concerned to analyse the origins of revolutionary terror. Serge recognised that the Bolsheviks were exercising a rule of terror in many ways comparable to that exercised in France during the Great Revolution in 1793-4. The exercise of such terror, and the repressive means used by the Bolshevik state inevitably aroused grave misgivings among anti-authoritarian revolutionaries in France. Serge shows clearly and concretely how the circumstances of the civil war and the ruthlessness of the revolution's enemies made such measures sadly but completely necessary. Even the most distasteful methods—such as using the wives and children of army officers as hostages in the event of their going over to the other side—are shown to be justified in the context of bitter all-out war. Yet there is an ambivalence about Serge's writings on terror that recalls some of the best writings of Rosa Luxemburg: a combination of the recognition of the necessity for revolutionary terror and a profound hatred of authoritarianism and violence. This ambivalence does not qualify Serge's defence of revolutionary terror; on the contrary it suggests that only those who recognise this ambivalence are entitled to actually exercise terror.

Serge's ambivalence was rooted in the very real contradictions of the revolution. For a revolution fighting for its very life, the terror and such instruments as the Cheka were a necessity. That does not require us to deny that specific actions of the Cheka manifested incompetence, overzealous sectarianism and pure vindictiveness. Serge knew that unless he compromised with Bolshevism he would be condemned to moralising impotence. Yet it was a real compromise, and it entailed contradictions that were not always easy to handle.

Serge himself later formulated the problem in terms of what he called the 'double duty' of the revolutionary, who must defend the revolution against both its external enemies and its own internal weaknesses.[19] So it is not surprising that a number of those who knew Serge during the early years of the revolution— the anarchists Gaston Leval and Mauricius, or the French communist Marcel Body who worked closely with Serge—testify to the fact that while his writings were solidly in support of the revolution, in private conversation with those he thought he could trust he made sharp criticisms of the Bolshevik regime. Leval quotes him as saying: 'We are obliged to lie to save what can be saved of the revolution.' [20]

Peter Sedgwick has written that 'the contrast is obvious between the Serge of libertarian reputation and the author of these manifestos for the elite leadership of the Bolsheviks'.[21] Certainly there are contradictions, but Sedgwick too easily ignores that there were libertarian as well as necessarily authoritarian currents in Bolshevism. There is a consistency in Serge's position, though it was one achieved at the price of considerable torment. Certainly Serge did not act out of cowardice or careerism; there were precious few material advantages to being a Bolshevik in the early years of the revolution, when even a small allocation of food seemed like a luxury. And when the time came Serge showed no lack of courage in supporting the Left Opposition. If he wrote in defence of Bolshevism, it was because he believed passionately that the revolution was worth defending.

The contradictions were at their most acute in the case of the Russian anarchists. All three pamphlets refer to anarchism and the third is devoted entirely to the subject. As one who had grown up in the anarchist tradition, Serge clearly felt a strong attachment but also a profound ambivalence towards anarchist politics. He saw anarchism as being a current within the revolutionary movement, one that had much to contribute, but only on condition that it played its part within the revolutionary process rather than standing outside in the name of an abstract purism.

However, the early years of the Russian revolution saw a continuing divergence between Bolsheviks and anarchists. Initially anarchists had co-operated closely; there were four anarchists— including Bill Shatov, who appears in Serge's account—on the Military Revolutionary Committee which organised the 1917 insurrection in Petrograd. A good number of anarchists joined the Bolsheviks or worked closely with them. But many anarchists opposed the Brest-Litovsk agreement, and in April 1919 Moscow anarchists staged an unnecessary provocation by stealing the car of a sympathetic American, Colonel Raymond Robins. The Cheka overreacted with a raid in which about forty anarchists were killed or wounded. In 1918 a group of anarchist Black Guards discussed seizing power in Moscow, and in 1919 anarchists bombed the headquarters of the Moscow Communist Party, killing twelve and injuring many more, including Bukharin.

Lenin's policy, repeated to various Russian and foreign anarchists, was that there should be full freedom for 'anarchists of ideas', but that those who organised armed resistance to Bolshevik rule would be repressed. In practice the distinction was very hard to make, and often the Cheka does not seem to have tried very hard to make it.[22]

Serge's plea for a fruitful synthesis of Bolshevism and anarchism seems to have been doomed to failure. In a highly confidential letter to the French syndicalist Michel Kneller, he wrote of the 'heart-breaking, indescribable bankruptcy of the

Russian anarchist movement', while deploring the 'absurd and criminal persecution'.[23] But Serge always maintained his contacts with anarchist circles; at the time of Kropotkin's funeral in 1921 he was the only party member to be seen as a comrade by the anarchists. He used his influence with the Bolsheviks to save anarchists from repression, notably helping to save the life of Voline, who had fought with Makhno in the Ukraine.[24]

In early 1921 the events at Kronstadt finally put an end to any hope of the sort of co-operation Serge advocated.[25] Yet even as late as 1938 Serge was still advocating a 'synthesis' of 'libertarian socialism' and 'scientific socialism',[26] still defending a socialism whose essence was human freedom.

These early pamphlets stand as a testimony to a moment at which the revolution was not yet lost, when the outcome still hung in the balance. In his depiction of the moral and material forces of the revolution, Serge reminds us that the defeat was not inevitable, that victory could have been generated out of the horrors of the early years of the revolution. His pamphlets will stand as an inspiration to those who aspire to emulate in the conditions of our own epoch the achievements of 1917—but with a very different outcome.

THESE WRITINGS were written and published in haste, and it is not surprising that a number of errors found their way into the published texts. I have corrected only what seem to be obvious misprints or mistakes about names and have otherwise tried to stay as close as possible to Serge's originals. For example, Serge may easily be forgiven his reference to 'Lord Churchill'; he had more important things on his mind than the subtleties of the British peerage system. Wherever possible, I have used the most familiar forms of Russian personal names, and the current modern forms of place names—thus Helsinki rather than Helsingfors. I have not attempted to preserve the eccentricities of Serge's punctuation.

SEVERAL PEOPLE helped me in completing this project. Richard Greeman, hard at work on the definitive biography of Serge, found time to give encouragement and stern criticism, both equally valuable. Mike Haynes assisted with some points of translation and Sharon O'Nions and Lovejeet Chand made useful comments on editing. The late Dave Widgery would never have allowed us to publish a volume by Serge without acknowledgement to the late Peter Sedgwick, who introduced so many of us to Serge in the sixties.

Ian Birchall
April 1997

NOTES

1   'Pendant la guerre civile', *Les Cahiers du travail* No 6, 15 May 1921; 'Les Anarchistes et l'expérience de la révolution russe', *Les Cahiers du travail* No 12, 15 August 1921.

2   'La Ville en danger', *La Vie ouvrière*, Nos 57-61 (4 June to 2 July, 1920); reprinted Paris, Librairie du travail, 1924. The 1924 version adds several sections not published in *La Vie ouvrière*, notably the introduction 'My Road to Russia' and the concluding section on Yudenich.

3   *La Ville en danger* was republished in the French reprint of *L'An I de la révolution russe* (Paris, 1971); *'Les Anarchistes...'* was reprinted in Alexandre Skirda's *Les Anarchistes dans la révolution russe* (Paris, 1975). As far as I know *Pendant la guerre civile* has never been republished.

4   A few pages from *La Ville en danger* are translated in D Cotterill (ed), *The Serge-Trotsky Papers* (London, 1994), pp 9-12.

5   Two pamphlets published by the Librairie du travail in 1925 are available in English. They are *What Everyone Should Know About State Repression* (London, 1979), and *Lenin in 1917* (*Revolutionary History*, vol 5 No 3 (1994), pp 3-53.

6   For example, in his *Memoirs* he wrote: 'I believe that the formation of the Chekas was one of the gravest and most impermissible errors that the Bolshevik leaders committed in 1918, when plots, blockades, and interventions made them lose their heads'. (*Memoirs of a Revolutionary*, Oxford, 1967, pp 80-81.)

7   Cited in Introduction to *Memoirs of a Revolutionary*, pp xviii-xix.

8   In an article on Martinet in *Les Humbles* Jan-Feb-March 1936 (special issue on Martinet); this article does not appear in Trotsky's

collected *Writings*.

9   See the account of an involved participant in A Rosmer, *Lenin's Moscow* (London, 1987).

10   From the article on Martinet cited in note 8.

11   Trotsky discusses his play *La Nuit* (The Night) in his essay 'A Drama of the French Working Class', *On Literature and Art* (New York, 1970), pp 148-61.

12   His novel *La Maison à l'abri* (The Sheltered House) was short-listed for the Prix Goncourt in 1919, the year it was won by Proust.

13   *Où va la révolution russe? L'affaire Victor Serge* (Paris, 1933).

14   M Gilbert, *Winston S Churchill*, vol. IV (London, 1975), pp 226-7.

15   W S Churchill, *The Second World War*, vol. VI (London, 1954), p 198.

16   *Manchester Guardian*, 13 July, 1920; cited in W P Coates & Z K Coates, *Armed Intervention in Russia 1918-1922*, (London, 1935), p 209.

17   *Armed Intervention in Russia*, p 229.

18   *Memoirs of a Revolutionary*, p 74.

19   V Serge, *Littérature et révolution* (Paris, 1976), p 77.

20   F Kupferman, *Au Pays des soviets* (Paris, 1979), p 41; see also Mauricius, *Au Pays des soviets* (Paris, 1921), p 197, M. Body, *Un Piano en bouleau de Carélie* (Paris, 1981), p 173.

21   P Sedgwick, 'The Unhappy Elitist: Victor Serge's Early Bolshevism', *History Workshop* No 17 (Spring 1984), p 151.

22   For an account that is sympathetic to the anarchists but does not deny their provocative behaviour, see P Avrich, *The Russian Anarchists* (Princeton N.J., 1967).

23   *The Serge-Trotsky Papers*, p 13.

24   *Memoirs of a Revolutionary*, pp 109-10, 123, 153.

25   This is not the place for an analysis of Serge's views on Kronstadt, at the time and subsequently. See *The Serge-Trotsky Papers*, pp 18-20, 150-191, 217-8.

26   V. Serge, *'La Pensée anarchiste'*, Crapouillot, January 1938, p 12.

Chronology

(all dates in the Gregorian calendar)

1917

7 November:	Bolsheviks take power in Petrograd
20 December:	Formation of Cheka

1918

3 March:	Brest-Litovsk Peace signed
11-12 April:	Cheka raid on Moscow anarchists
2 August:	Allied forces occupy Archangel
11 November:	Armistice—end of World War I

1919

15 January:	Murder of Luxemburg and Liebknecht
February:	Serge arrives in Petrograd
2-7 March:	First Congress of Communist International
21 March:	Soviet rule in Hungary
May:	Beginning of Yudenich's offensive against Petrograd
1 August:	Collapse of Hungarian Soviet Republic
25 September:	Anarchists bomb Moscow Communist headquarters
11-22 October:	Yudenich starts drive on Petrograd: pushed back

1920

14 November:	Wrangel evacuates Crimea —end of civil war
26 November:	Red Army attacks Makhno

1921

13 February:	Funeral of Kropotkin
2-17 March:	Kronstadt Rising
3-19 July:	Founding Congress of Red International of Labour Unions

During the civil war

Petrograd: May-June 1919 Impressions and considerations

other people will write the history of the civil war and theorise about it. In these brief notes, hastily put down on paper at a time when we scarcely had the leisure to keep a diary, and completed later with hindsight, my aim is above all to paint a picture, to sketch a few portraits, to conjure up the atmosphere of some of the gravest hours that the Russian revolution lived through. I hope that these pages will be of value to militants who did not themselves experience the social war and find it hard to imagine it. Certain necessities of struggle, which it is always difficult to accept in the abstract, stand out clearly just as they followed logically from the events. It is a question, as always, of revolutionary terror, which you can only understand if you have seen it growing irresistibly out of the surrounding circumstances, as one of the most unavoidable manifestations of the laws of history. It is a question, too, of the necessity of dictatorship and of revolutionary defence.

25 MAY 1919

Towards the end of May 1919 there was nothing to indicate that new battles in the civil war were imminent. The counter-revolutionary elements in the Petrograd population were cherishing great hopes, but they did not make them public. The attention of the Communists was mainly fixed on the eastern front, where Kolchak was threatening the Volga region, and on the unstable situation in the Ukraine, ravaged by the anti-Semitic forces and demoralised by bad Communists, against whom draconian measures were about to be taken. Petrograd was calm, although from time to time there was talk of an impending Finnish attack. We had talked about it so much without seeing anything materialise that we ended up by no longer believing in it. Moreover, we were confirmed in our feeling of confidence by certain excellent arguments. If the Finns had occupied Petrograd, they would have to feed it: something that would have been difficult for a country that was itself subject to rationing, despite the economic support it was getting from the Entente. It would have been necessary to set up a White government, and that would have meant a monarchist government which, one way or the other, would have refused to recognise the total independence of Finland; and finally it would have been necessary to mount a prolonged defence of the Red capital against the revolutionary armies. So common sense boosted our feeling of confidence. And indeed we needed quite a strong dose of it to resist the unhealthy atmosphere prevailing in certain circles.

A few days before the onset of the tragedy I happened to meet some people of my acquaintance who were 'Whites'. For it is one of the peculiarities of civil war that 'Reds' and 'Whites' rub shoulders with each other and are acquainted; there are even families divided between the two camps where personal affection does not disappear completely. In a street in Petrograd which used to be 'bourgeois', three neighbours from the district had stopped to talk in low voices: they were a shopkeeper, a doctor and a chemist. They greeted me in a friendly fashion. And it was basically with the intention of doing me a good turn that the doctor told me in a confidential tone that major events were about to happen: 'This time, the British will certainly be there. And perhaps the Finns. They're giving details such as. . . I advise you to look after yourself.'

The shopkeeper tried to outdo him: 'Apparently last night the gunfire from Kronstadt could be heard quite clearly. And you realise that Kronstadt can't hold out for long against the British.'

I didn't believe them—and I was sceptical of news coming from such a source. I had rapidly learnt the nature of this little world of intellectuals calling themselves liberals, socialists and even revolutionaries (before the revolution became a social one). I knew how pitifully incapable of action they were. I went on my way. They remained on the pavement—a shopkeeper, a doctor, a chemist—three likeable but anachronistic figures with their threadbare overcoats, their dubious detachable collars and their bowler hats. Ever since, that trio seen on a May evening in 1919 has stuck in my memory, like a symbol. The whole bourgeois population, which was being crushed by the formidable millstones of the dictatorship of the proletariat, was still anxiously looking forward to the collapse of the still shaky Communist regime, which was betrayed on all sides and undermined by innumerable hatreds. For these people embodied hatred and sabotage. The shopkeeper was a speculator; I found out not long afterwards that he had sold a house in Petrograd (this kind of speculation on real estate in the large Russian cities was actually thriving in Finland). The chemist ran a dispensary and every evening brought back from his work anecdotes which were both hilarious and sinister. For essential medical supplies were unavailable and they were replaced by whatever means were possible: a few wretches gave free play to their imagination with tricks which were sometimes criminal. Negligence, disorder, sabotage, theft and speculation were arranged in a variety of combinations. Alcohol intended for medical purposes was sold at 15,000 roubles for a small bottle. Narcotics such as cola-nuts and cocaine vanished in the same way. And the manager of the Communist dispensary said with a little smile: 'What do you expect? It's what you get with nationalisation!' As for the doctor, he did nothing at all since he 'couldn't be expected to work with Bolsheviks'. 'Besides,' he added, 'it won't last long. It only remains to bury the corpse of Bolshevism.' The most peculiar thing, and also the saddest, was that these three men prided themselves on not being reactionaries. One of them used to tell, with a certain pride, how during the February revolution he had participated in the capture of the police station in his district, and in the organisation of the citizens' militia. During those same days the doctor had risked his life several times hunting down the remaining policemen of the old regime who had taken refuge in attics with machine-guns.

In the great Red city, conquered by the workers, there were at that time about six or seven thousand Communist Party members and less than a hundred thousand workers; for already the youngest and most energetic among the workers had gone to the front. The remainder of the population (that is, about seven eighths) were either politically indifferent—passive—or hostile. This was the mass of 'townspeople'—to make a not very satisfactory translation of the Russian word *obyvatel*, which indicates the mass of fearful, discontented and backward people. It was on this mass, cowardly and wretched but angry, that the reactionaries placed their hopes. What did they spend their time on? Almost exclusively on speculation, that is, unauthorised trade. In short, the shopkeepers, traders, businessmen and intellectuals were quite determined to carry on with business as usual, taking no account of the soviet regime. And even the slightest measures decreed by the soviet came up against the underhand resistance of a generalised ill will, but without any sign of open opposition. Everywhere, each evening, there were the same conversations in low voices about Allied intervention, about the collapse of the Communists and the massacre that would follow. Naturally nobody actually wanted this massacre to take place, but everybody expected it. The doctor sighed: 'Our people are so uncultivated, what do you expect!' And his friends and followers 'took note of the progress of anti-Semitism and of the loathing felt for the Bolsheviks'. In the marketplace and in the queues outside the bakeries the gossips passed on 'guaranteed information' about the 'pogrom due next Sunday'. I remember the charming six-year-old daughter of one of my Jewish friends who came home from school one day crying because the other children had told her that 'at last the Yids were going to get their guts cut out'.

That was the enemy, the counter-revolution, all these things which cannot be portrayed or described briefly, for they sprang from ignorance, stupidity, cowardice, moral bankruptcy, the embittered egoism of the entire population of a city which had been profoundly corrupted by the capitalist system. We could feel it all around us, on the watch, looking for our weaknesses, our mistakes, our follies, skilfully making us stumble, ready at the slightest lapse to pounce on us and tear us to pieces. But although in the town we were, in purely numerical terms, only a small minority, we still felt that in face of the enemy we represented vigour, the only living vigour. For on our side, and on our side alone, we had thought, idealism, will, daring, dedication. And despite everything, from a certain point of view we had an impressive numerical superiority. For the six thousand Communists constituted merely the most active element on the 'Red' side. Behind them, sympathising instinctively with the party and carrying out all the menial tasks required by the revolution, there were sixty to eighty thousand working men and women, ready for any sacrifice in the event of real danger. The 'Whites', despite being so numerous in the city, had neither such a minority capable of taking initiatives, nor any such reserves to draw on.

It is impossible to understand anything of the history of the civil war without picturing these two opposing forces, mingled together, sharing the same life, rubbing shoulders in the thoroughfares of the cities with the constant, clear recognition that one side would have to kill the other. They were well aware of it, the three intellectuals talking in lowered voices on the corner of Voznesensky Prospect; while the sailor who walked by, casting a distrustful look in their direction, and the working woman, her head covered with an old coloured handkerchief, who stared nonchalantly at them—these two, being 'Reds', were aware of it too.

29–30 MAY 1919

These Whites and Reds can live alongside each other for some time without any open display of hatred, rubbing shoulders almost fraternally. Yesterday they were all busy in the same way, in pursuit of nourishment and entertainment. In these times of shortage everyone's primary concern was to obtain bread or potatoes for the next day. Once that was done, some went to the theatre or the cinema, some to clubs, some to party meetings, some to lectures or poetry readings. Our fifteen theatres, our thirty cinemas (managed by the state), our five or six daily concerts—not to speak of numerous evening classes—were not sufficient for the needs of a crowd greedy for relaxation and sensation, and which did not seek the noisy idleness of cafés—and a good thing too. Even yesterday you could have believed that this was all that life involved, normal life, as people of a calm disposition might call it.

But this morning the city was beset with great anxiety. The Whites and the Reds were eyeing each other, their faces inscrutable, their look obstinate and deliberately expressionless. This morning I learnt of the heroic death of Tolmachev, of the murder at the front of a handful of Communists, and of the way that the Whites suddenly and treacherously attacked the Reds. Not many miles from our intelligent Petrograd, devoted to music and ideas, this was a mediaeval slaughter, like those described by Philippe de Commines in his chronicles, when the men of Burgundy and Picardy, the English and the French, the followers of the King and of Charles the Bold set ambushes for each other at the turning of the road, or invited each other to drink so that they might be better able to cut each other's throats at the end of the orgy, amid overturned torches and wild cries of 'Kill! Kill!'

Yes, this was done on this 29 May, just outside the walls of Petrograd.

The details of this sombre drama reached us at the very same time as the news of the death of Tolmachev, who had died three days earlier. Surrounded by the Whites in the Luga Upland, not far from the hamlet of the Red Mountains, a few stubborn soldiers fought to the death around Tolmachev, who blew his brains out at the last moment. The nature of this war is such that the 'Reds' do not surrender: in fact, in general neither side takes prisoners among non-commissioned officers. If Red commissars, militants or commandants are taken by surprise they are invariably shot. For our part we don't spare former officers, or non-commissioned officers of any sort. War to the death with no humanitarian hypocrisy; there is no Red Cross and stretcher-bearers are not allowed. Primitive warfare, war of extermination, *civil war*.

Tolmachev, whose pistol shot is echoing around Petrograd today with the fateful sound of an alarm bell, died at the age of twenty-three. He was a student who joined the Bolsheviks at the age of eighteen. During the war he became a factory worker as the best means of agitation. He was a member of the executive committee of the Communist Party in Petrograd during the period of clandestine activity; he participated in the February and October revolutions, and worked as a propagandist first in the Petrograd tram garages and then in the factories of the Urals. He was an implacable, and successful, opponent of the Social Revolutionaries, of the Mensheviks and of patriots of every hue in the Urals, which had not been fully won over to soviet rule. Finally he became commissar of the little army which stood up to the Cossack Dutov, in the Don country; then deputy commander of the army on the Siberian front during the Czechoslovak offensive; then commissar of a unit hastily dispatched to Yamburg to protect Petrograd, where he fell in the middle of the battle. His short life as a revolutionary leaves an epic memory. There can have been few men, even in a period so fertile in deeds as this one, who have, in such a short space of time, lived so feverishly and expended so much energy in sacrificing themselves ceaselessly, in fighting, in improvising the new law, the new force, in multiplying sacrifice and victory, from Petrograd to the mountains of Siberia, from the Urals to the Don!

At least he did not die as a result of treachery. The death of the others, of those murdered on 29 May—Tavrin, Kupche, Rakov and his wife—was truly atrocious.

They were at rest, sleeping in a peasant's *isba* (wooden hut). Two battalions were occupying a village near Yamburg; they were in the middle of a campaign. At dawn they were due to spread out in assault waves. Someone crept through the dark streets of the sleeping village. Someone knocked on the windows. The doors suddenly flew open and there were shouts. The Whites were there, with grenades in their hands. The sentries had betrayed, or having been themselves betrayed, were dead. And it was the Red deputy commander, a wretch called Zaitsev who, having fixed the epaulettes of the old regime onto his black leather tunic, was leading the Whites. The Red commanding officers—almost all of them formerly officers of the Tsarist guard—were triumphant. They embraced each other as though a nightmare were ending. But the nightmare was only just beginning. On the threshold of a hut, the Communist commander of the regiment, Tavrin, appeared. He was knocked down with a bullet and finished off with a sabre. Then he was stripped—for clothing is scarce—his property was shared out, his body was chopped up with a sabre, one of his ears was cut off and his tongue was torn out. Then a hunt for Communists began. Commissar Kupche was found by a 'Communist' officer who tore up his party card under his nose, shouting 'Now you scum are done for!' Kupche was cold-bloodedly stripped of his clothes and shot before his wife's eyes. Rakov, the brigade commissar, was left alone to defend himself desperately. He barricaded himself into a peasant house, and they only managed to kill him when his machine-gun broke. The battalion commissars were shot one after the other. Then the men lined up and marched past their new leaders to the sound of the march of the Semionovsky regiment. Doubtless these men had previously been worn down by a propaganda effort. The surprise and fear of the majority, combined with the treachery of a few, meant that a whole regiment went over to the enemy. A great victory was proclaimed in the capitals of the civilised world. But the very same evening forty men deserted and went back to the Reds.

Now the White army is hastening towards Petrograd, which Denikin's newspapers are already announcing as captured. Panic-stricken rumours are circulating in the city. The Whites who are living among us can scarcely conceal their joy. Ah! They've really won the game this time.

We are given lists of the names of regiments which have gone over to the enemy. The Red army is collapsing. 'Jewish rule' is at an end!

The fact is that the Whites are just outside Gatchina. Zinoviev urges all the northern towns to send detachments 'which may be weak but must be experienced' to assist Petrograd. 'Comrades, hasten, for every hour is precious. Leave everything else till later. Petrograd must be saved at all costs.'

2-4 JUNE 1919

After a miraculous escape from the bullets of the firing squad, the wife of commissar Kupche has returned to Petrograd. After the execution of her husband—from whom she was separated only a few moments before his death—she was taken away together with the wives of several other Reds. Their fate was not yet settled, though it seemed almost certain. The next morning they were lined up at the edge of a wood and told to take their clothes off. They understood what would happen to them. Comrade Kupche fell beneath the bullets of the White guns, miraculously unscathed, while all the other women lay dead. The executioners did not bother to finish off their victims, being quite certain that no human assistance could come to them. Comrade Kupche reached our outposts virtually naked—having kept nothing but a ragged shirt—her feet lacerated and starving with hunger. She is a small woman with brown hair, very unaffected; she speaks softly, almost in a whisper, and when she speaks you would think something inside her was broken. In her pale face her eyes are anguished, with a look of exhaustion.

The White army is gathering outside Petrograd. Everywhere it has gone it has left a trail of blood behind it. Certainly during the Great War men of all nations fell in some very squalid barbarities. But I don't think that ever, anywhere, the contempt for life and for human suffering have been systematically developed in such a degraded fashion. A few miles from a civilised city, prisoners are being wantonly murdered. Our newspapers are full of such stories—whose authenticity I can vouch for—and in fact they give only a very weak impression of the horror of what is going on. 'All Jews, Communists and former officers fall out!' That was the formula used. Torture, hanging, shooting, slaughter with cold steel, beatings and sham trials—these were the alternative outcomes. As for the Red soldiers who were taken prisoner, they were simply sent to the rear for a few days, long enough to give them new officers and to make them march against us—willingly or under compulsion.

The law is: kill or be killed. I know very well that if the Whites enter the city all those who are dear to me can expect no mercy. Everyone knows this as well as I do. The air is permeated with a vague smell of blood, creating among us a state of mind in which terror cannot fail to grow. We can sense the approach of terror just as before thunderstorms you can feel the air charged with electricity.

On 31 May *Pravda* carried two significant and terrible paragraphs: 'Death to Spies!' Lenin and Dzerzhinsky have addressed an appeal to everyone to be vigilant in stamping out espionage. Fortunately we are in no way predisposed to spy mania. Otherwise the situation would be very grave. For in time of civil war the spy can be virtually anyone. But perhaps just because the terrible threat hangs over everyone, it has to remain, and in fact generally does remain, ineffective. Nonetheless it is a direct order to show no pity. And in such circumstances such an order must be taken quite literally. On the third page of the same issue of the official organ of the Communist party, the Revolutionary Tribunal of the Third Army announces: *deserters will be shot.* 'Several dozen deserters, fugitives, looters and spreaders of panic have been punished with all the severity that traitors deserve.' 'We were defeated near Yamburg because all the comrades of the Red army have not yet acquired, to an equal degree, the sense of duty towards the working class and the revolution.' Why does the revolution also have to have recourse to this sickening use of military force? We don't ask about that any more. This is not the time for arguments. The revolution is at war. If it doesn't suppress panic, the physical cowardice of the masses at certain times, the demented, cowardly selfishness of individuals, then it is lost: and its loss will mean that the blood of these same people will flow in huge quantities.

The treachery of the Semenov regiment—which was not an isolated occurrence—has borne fruit. The Special Commission (the Cheka) has published a list of twelve people, most of them women, belonging to the families of the officers of the Third Regiment of fusiliers, which shamefully went over to the enemy; these twelve have been arrested as hostages. The same commission has announced that it has shot twenty-seven people: seven Whites, all former officers, one of whom held a position of trust in the Red army, the captain of a destroyer and his senior officers; three accomplices of the *ataman* Bulak-Balakhovich who went over to the Whites with a whole detachment of cavalry and who today is notorious for his atrocities; the eight thieves who stole a lorry load of sugar belonging to the City Food Committee.

8 JUNE 1919

The life of our fine hungry city, which is a battlefield, does not stop for a second. Hunger is permanently established in at least 300,000 homes; anxiety is everywhere. Like tunnels dug in opposing directions, mingled in the depths of the soil, treachery, plots and terror pursue each other all around us, amongst us. Queues of fifty to a hundred people stand outside the bakeries where the commune distributes to everybody the bread it has available. The same day, I heard the commissar in charge of supplies, the athletic Badayev, who was a deputy in the Duma and then a convict in Siberia, say with a frown: 'I have reserves for less than four days'; and a comrade from the Special Commission added , '...within a week the Whites will try something at the rear.' The same evening, I stopped by a canal with a group of idlers who were watching British aeroplanes manoeuvring above us. In the distance we could hear explosions. A woman told us that the previous day railway workers had been killed by a bomb at the station; a sailor spoke to us about the fire at the Kronstadt supply depot which was still burning. It was a light, mild evening, and we were outside a smart gardening shop.

For despite everything life goes on. Perhaps we shall be slaughtered tomorrow; that doesn't matter. The main thing is to keep calm and resolute today, and to be able to think of something else from time to time. Today, Sunday, during the funerals of Tolmachev, Rakov, Kupche and Tavrin, there was an artistic oasis amid the sorrowful and threatened city. Hundreds of people came to the small white hall of the Conservatory to listen to music by Glazunov. The great composer was there himself, tall and stooping, his broad shoulders gaunt, with pallor, weariness and anaemia visible in the heavy creases of his face. For, though he is a great artist, he is not one of those who fiddle things in order to live comfortably during these days of starvation. The blockade creates three main categories of victims: children, old people, and artists and scholars—three vulnerable groups whom we strive to protect (but how is it possible to save them all?). It was a charming morning of good music. There was a young woman, blonde, graceful and slender like a Greek statue, a wonderful artist. For a long time she too held this audience charmed by her violin-playing. Then, in a smart black dress-coat, as though at a fashionable reception in the old days, Maximov sang Heine's *Lieder*.

One day, when these things are discussed with a concern for justice and truth, when, in the society of the future that we shall ultimately build, where all the wounds of humanity will have been healed, then the revolution will be praised because it never, even in its most tragic days, lost the concern for art; it never neglected rhythms, fine gestures, beautiful voices full of pathos, dream-like settings, poems, anthems played on the organ, the sobbing notes of violins. Never. And I cannot help discovering in this obstinate quest for beauty, at every hour of the civil war, stoicism, strength and confidence. Doubtless it is because the Red city is suffering and fighting so that one day leisure and art shall be the property of all.

Certainly no other city at war has the solemn countenance of Petrograd today. Elsewhere often even under shellfire you find musical cafés, drunkenness, women dolled up in bars to distract those whose job it is to kill others or to get themselves killed. Here, on this grey, rainy Sunday I have seen only two things—and I have travelled all over the city—art and mourning.

It is an austere mourning. In an almost deserted street—there is very little movement on Sundays, outside the main thoroughfares—I met Communists who were going to the funeral. Young men and women, all with similar clothes and similar hair-styles, in military dress of greenish brown and black leather, with revolvers at their side and red flags in their hands—each group of brave young people looks the same, with candid faces in many of which there is still something childlike.

We shall not be destroyed! This soul of the revolutionary city contains too much beauty, this flesh and blood of the city contain too much energy!

10 JUNE 1919

Lull. Yudenich is forty miles away at the most. The situation is imperceptibly getting ever more tense. Work carries on without excessive excitement, and the roads show the normal signs of life. Just now, not far from the Warsaw Station, at the exact spot where, in July 1904, Sazonov's bomb blew Plehve's carriage* to pieces, I passed a regiment on its way to the front, that is, to the outer suburbs. Women and friends were mingling with the soldiers, carrying their haversacks. Pitiable faces on the verge of separation, with trembling lips and swollen eyelids—and often they were trying very hard to still look brave! Men no longer go off to the front drunk, singing patriotic songs, with panic in their hearts and madness in their brains. That was all right for the other war, for the insane war. This one, where they understand why they are fighting, is a dirty job, nothing more, which they accept without weakness—but with sadness, because now it's not a question of being soldiers but simply of being men.

---

* The Social Revolutionary Sazonov assassinated the Tsar's Prime Minister von Plehve. *[Translator's note]*

Further on, young men are training in the street. At a given signal the groups of kneeling men jump up, spread out and advance towards an imaginary enemy. Three lads have just taken shelter behind a pile of sand that has been brought here for some maintenance work. They are laughing. A worker stops to tell them his experiences as a former soldier.

This evening at the Great Dramatic Theatre, Smirnova dances. She is slender, sinewy and graceful, and seems to be carried away by the rhythms that surround her. They perform a scene from *l'Arlésienne*, Glazunov's *Salome*, and an exquisite little piece called *Liebesleid* (sufferings of love), melancholy and luminous.

On the Karelian front, White bands have appeared. If a serious attack were launched in the north, we could well be lost.

12 JUNE 1919

The Red city knows nothing as yet. But it is on the very verge of disaster.

This evening's *Izvestia* announces that tomorrow, at the People's Hall, there will be a meeting to mark the funeral ceremonies for Karl Liebknecht and Rosa Luxemburg. An instruction from Trotsky, countersigned by Zinoviev, is published on the front page: 'You are instructed to establish the family situation of all former officers who have been integrated into the command structure of the Red army and to inform them that the consequences of any treachery will fall on their families. Make all former officers sign a statement that they have received this information.' This precautionary measure, agreed a long time ago, had never been put into practice. For it is important to stress that the measures enforced by the revolution, terrible as some of them may be, have been made necessary by the audacity, perseverance, and unscrupulousness of its enemies. This manner of taking hostages is necessitated by the relentless amorality of the civil war. When White officers kill our soldiers do they think of the families of those whom they are killing?

All Communists have been told to assemble at seven o'clock, by the sector (or administrative district) committees of the city. The instruction has been spread by word of mouth. Between

seven o'clock and eight or nine, quite a crowd assembles outside
the various party premises. It is made up of working men and
women, office workers, and a number of young women. In this
district where I live, about two thousand people have responded to
the call, without being very sure what it is all about. Shall we have
to take arms? People are ready to do so, without any visible
display of nerves. The crowd arranges itself, splits up and gets
organised, something which is quite difficult, after much tramping
about on the deserted square—for under martial law nobody is
allowed to move around the streets after eight o'clock at night.
The party committees issue special permits which are valid for
three days. Around eleven, soldiers and sailors arrive, in an orderly
fashion with rifles on their shoulders. Among the soldiers, in the
front row, I notice the long hair of a proletarian poet who is
highly rated in Communist circles. Here it is party members who
occupy positions of responsibility, so important officials from the
administration, well-known agitators and commissars are to be
found alongside labourers and women who are employed in their
offices. News is passed on in a whisper: the Kronstadt forts have
been handed over to the Whites by an act of treachery, the
Krasnaia Gorka fort, the only defence for Petrograd, on the coast,
is in the hands of traitors who are flying the White flag. I dare not
believe that these things are true. Doubtless they are
exaggerations, as always. For if it's true... At midnight the
Communists are finishing organising themselves into squads, each
of which must contain two armed men, soldiers or sailors, two
women and several helpers; meanwhile, in a small hall in the
Committee building, a pale, thin young man is reading aloud the
instruction on house-to-house searches. And I find out that the
rumours are true.

The comrade who tells me this has just come from Smolny.
He has seen Zinoviev. Over there, people are very worried.

'So,' I ask, 'is this the end?'

My acquaintance shrugs his shoulders.

'Nonsense! We'll hold out again this time!'

This is the dominant attitude in people's minds. Nobody
believes that the situation is as serious as it is. They've seen it all
before. They feel confident, with a certain casualness; after all,

that is the state of mind of victors, albeit exhausted victors.

A sleepless midnight. A limpid, rather pale twilight gives a faint blue tinge to the far ends of the streets. You might think it was morning, very early morning. The squads set off. We hear their footsteps, lively but harsh, on the paving stones. They have to disarm the Whites in a single night. There must not be one gun left in the attics, the cellars and the private apartments. Twelve thousand Communists and sympathisers (recruited exclusively among working people) are taking part in these house-to-house searches. In the 'White' districts, that is, all the districts that are not exclusively inhabited by poor people, houses are ransacked, room by room. The inhabitants' papers are examined. Rifle-butts echo on the thresholds. The squads of civilians and soldiers, in which men and women of all ages are mixed together, are like bands of insurgents. And that is what they are. Insurgents, who tomorrow will be shot, every single one of them, if today they spare those who are spying on them from innocent-seeming rooms out of the windows of which automatic pistols and Nagant revolvers are being thrown. Bill-posters are going through every street pasting up an order signed Peters: 'All weapons remaining in the hands of individuals must be surrendered within twenty-four hours, on pain of death.'

Nothing out of the ordinary has yet happened in this peaceful district of Petrograd. But nonetheless there is often a very clear sense that these are decisive hours. The white light of night seems to become colder and paler; the lifeless streets seem strangely empty; it appears that the city is holding its breath, in the expectation of a sudden outcome.

The telephones are ringing. At the Committee headquarters, some bits of fragmentary conversation are still echoing in my ears.

'There's no petrol for the armoured cars. The seventeen bourgeois who have been arrested...' Out in the street, two squads pass, and stop to talk for a minute. 'Kronstadt is on fire...the fleet is deciding what to do...' they say. But they know nothing precise, except that things are happening from one minute to the next.

Three o'clock in the morning. It is light, as on a slightly misty morning, light and cold. Outside a house which is being searched, a young soldier and a schoolgirl are laughing and smoking. Through the window I can see a family group sitting beneath a hanging lamp which has just been switched on, and for some reason the contrast between the electric light and the pale daylight makes me feel sad. There is an old woman and some girls. A sailor has gone up to them, is reading their identity papers, then looking carefully round the room, examining the chests of drawers, the couch, the heavy furniture where a gun could be concealed.

There is a sudden din of heavy motor lorries passing over the uneven paving of the road. Two go by, bristling with bayonets. Sailors and civilians are standing up in them, their rifles held upright. They're going somewhere as reinforcements.

13 JUNE 1919

At Smolny, just now, a comrade from the executive committee of the soviet was giving a vivid account of her inspection visit to the front line the previous night, and how she had had a battery of light artillery urgently moved. This militant, who now holds an important position of responsibility, used to be a tailoring worker. Her simplicity has been supplemented by a great seriousness, a sort of gravity. Her improvised strategy is probably better than that of a highly trained specialist who sympathises with the enemy.

The day is calm, despite our anxieties. The battle remains undecided. Now I know the whole truth of the situation, which the city as yet knows only through vague rumours. A fort at Kronstadt has been blown up. Two ships from the war fleet have tried to go over to the Whites; I don't know whether they succeeded or not. The fortress of Krasnaia Gorka is in the hands of the Whites, as well as the radio station. Those occupying it have transmitted a message to the British fleet and to the Finnish government, to ask for their assistance and promising them a rapid victory. The Yudenich offensive is finally developing to the west and south within a maximum radius of less than forty miles. In short, Petrograd is threatened on all sides. By sea, where the British can take action from one moment to the next (their planes are bombing Kronstadt and sometimes Petrograd), and where

units of the Baltic fleet may well be flying the flag of counter-
revolution; by the ever watchful Finland, which has already
unleashed its Karelian volunteers against us, and which is
vociferously demanding Izhora Land, that is, the whole of the
mouth of the Neva; by the White and Estonian forces (Yudenich,
Rodzianko, Balakhovich) to the South and West. But the worst
danger is certainly that from within. It is everywhere. Is there a
conspiracy, on a wide scale or more limited? Certainly all these
treacheries—the Semenov regiment, the Krasnaia Gorka, the
Pavel fort, the battleships *Petropavlosk* and *Andrei Pervozvanny*—fit
together and are connected, giving a clear impression of
something planned in advance. Have we reached the end of the
list yet? Who will betray next? Which fort, which battleship,
which headquarters? Two thirds of the officers in the army and
the fleet served under the old regime; three quarters of the
intellectuals and civil servants 'sabotaged' the social revolution for
as long as they could, and will carry on doing so. At the lowest
estimate there are a hundred thousand Whites in Petrograd
around us and among us, if you define as a 'White' any citizen
who detests us, who fervently desires the re-establishment of
private property by the Allied forces and the punishment of the
Communists. This evening, tomorrow at the latest, we shall know
for sure.

Meanwhile, the weather is fine. At around six o'clock, the
pathways on the Kronversky Prospect, behind the Peter-Paul
Fortress, are filling up with people. Soon quite a crowd is
streaming towards the huge iron-built theatre of the House of the
People, where the meeting in honour of Rosa Luxemburg and
Karl Liebknecht is due to be held. Zinoviev is billed to speak.
People are keen to hear the truth about the situation from his
mouth. Trainee soldiers arrive, carrying their flags. Then whole
companies of soldiers appear. The hall is an enormous iron
framework, in which there are several balconies one above the
other, overlooking a tiered pit; it is flooded by a huge crowd. How
many faces will be there in the sad grey daylight? Four thousand,
six thousand, no less, and probably more. An impressive sight.
Iron, nothing but iron, beams, pillars, girders, rope-moulding, all
in taut iron—and below men, soldiers, workers, young women, it

seems like the whole population of the streets of Petrograd in Year Two brought into this one place; the crowd is hardly tumultuous, despite all those raised foreheads and watchful eyes. Seen from the platform, the living half-light of this hall is like an abyss. This blurred, multiplied humanity, raised up, held and imprisoned in the magnificent metallic edifice that it has built for itself, this humanity, which is anxious and pained, keeps silent as it awaits the words that will be thrown down to it from here; suddenly I feel I can measure its elemental force.

Three speeches in particular made a visible impact on the crowd, although it also applauded Hungarian and German comrades who had come to bring fraternal greetings from European revolutionaries. Peters was the first to speak. Abroad Peters is cloaked in a sinister mythology, fabricated by a rather dubious type of journalism which is expert at exploiting news stories; in fact he is an ordinary young man in a grey suit. To tell the truth, his appearance is not very prepossessing, and he doesn't smile much. His face has thick, rather harsh features, he looks somewhat sullen, like a bulldog, with pale grey eyes. He pronounces clearly, but with a Latvian accent. He begins his speech by declaring in a loud voice: 'A people always finds its Judas! Judas! Judas! Since treachery is everywhere, let it be quite clear that we shall crush it without fail, ruthlessly'. Six thousand people welcome this threat with cheers. If, later on, the newspapers in London and Paris accuse Peters of being responsible for the Red terror, they will be lying. I saw terror voted by acclamation by the people of Petrograd, coming up from the streets, freely, at the call of danger.

The next speaker was Antselovich, young, full-blooded, with a warm voice and vigorous gestures; he listed the sacrifices made by revolutionary Germany and named the martyrs. Zinoviev appeared only at the end. When he was seen on the platform, a member of the party Bureau whispered to me: 'That's a good sign! The battle of Krasnaia Gorka must be going our way.' And that was indeed the case. Zinoviev gave some detailed information on the events that had taken place. Within a few hours, we should have recaptured Krasnaia Gorka. But while he was speaking, a clicking sound, like clockwork suddenly being set in motion, could be heard to the left, in the wings. For this platform is a stage. The same thought immediately occurred to all of us. Peters rushed off, as did others, including me. The speaker never turned a hair, though he heard the noise and signalled to us. We didn't find anything. But from now on I was fully aware that the breast of this man who was speaking, tribune of the class war, was exposed to the enemy's blows. Then the whole hall echoed with cheers and a magnificent chorus gave voice to *the Internationale*.

As we came out, we could hear gunfire.

NIGHT OF 13 JUNE 1919

The heavy, dull sound of shelling continues to echo in the distance at brief intervals. Doubtless it comes from Krasnaia Gorka. Each shot reminds us that the position is still in the hands of the Whites. They are holding out. From one hour to the next, the Finnish—or British—attack may be launched. On this sleepless night, the city is awake for its armed vigil. The house-to-house searches continue. But the voluntary surrender of weapons has exceeded all expectations. In all the party committee buildings, in all the militia offices, whole rooms are full of rifles, revolvers and sabres, piled up as though after a battle. But here it is before the battle that they have been removed from the enemy. Those who bring weapons are not asked for any explanation. Those in whose houses weapons are found, after repeated warnings and the extension of the period for surrendering arms *on pain of death*, are arrested on the spot. At the headquarters of the Special Commission (Cheka), a brand new German machine-gun has been brought in, found in a private house. It is not the first. In the cellars of a consulate (the Romanian, I think), I am told they have found a small naval gun.

The street is ready to become a battlefield. The preparations taken in the pale light of nighttime have a sort of solemnity about them. Motorcycles, armed with machineguns, set off through the deserted streets. Armoured cars await a signal. In the entrance halls of the committee buildings, machineguns have been placed. Groups of militia men and Communists, with bayonets fixed to their guns, are gathering in the Gorkhovaia, at the doors of the militia headquarters.

18-19 JUNE 1919

Ever since 14 June, although the situation remained very serious and no significant change had occurred, we had the sense that the crisis was over. It may well have simply been a relaxation of the nerves. But however that may be, the shelling stopped on 14 June, although the Whites held the Krasnaia Gorka fort until the night of 16 June. On the sixteenth, towards midnight, the sailors from Kronstadt mounted an assault on the fort which the Red fleet had shelled. The garrison put up only a feeble resistance. A number of soldiers who had been taken by surprise by the treachery of the White officers remained passive, not wishing to fight against the Reds. The officers and a small minority of the gunners—those who had condemned themselves by shelling Kronstadt and the surrounding villages—resisted ferociously. No revolutionary court will have to spend time judging them. The sailors, during the assault, did not bother with such formalities.

The conspiracy—or the conspiracies—are turning out to be vast and complex. They result from the tension built up by all the hatred against the Reds. The objective aimed at was the capture of Petrograd, with the assistance of the British fleet, assistance which decisive events in the interior of the country would have made extremely probable (and which, moreover, had perhaps even been promised). In the Petrograd region, the initiative lay with the former army and navy officers, in collusion with the 'Union for the Regeneration of Russia' and the 'National Centre', made up of the Constitutional Democrats, the Right Social Revolutionaries and Denikin. Thus the ramifications of the White organisations stretch into the south with Denikin and into Siberia with Kolchak, to Finland and Estonia, to the White army of Yudenich and Rodzianko, to the British fleet and to the Allied intelligence agencies at Helsinki and Tallinn. Documents prove the involvement of the Mensheviks and the *oborontsi* (patriots, Plekhanov's former group) in the conspiracy. The Right Social Revolutionaries were of course involved, and some lost sheep from the 'Left' Social Revolutionaries too. The movement was set in motion a little prematurely as a result of the explosion (on the morning of 12 June) at the Pavel fort. The signal was supposed to be given from Krasnaia Gorka. Most of the Kronstadt forts and two battleships (the *Andrei Pervozvanny* and the *Petropavlosk*) had more or less gone over to the Whites, as well as several military headquarters in Petrograd and Krasnoe Selo. And according to a plan meticulously prepared in advance, a few hours of treachery could have made Petrograd over to the Whites.

The Krasnaia Gorka officers, led by Major Nekludov, were ahead of time, and since they were not followed by the troops and the crews—on the two battleships said to have 'gone over' there was no more than a momentary hesitation—they were defeated. What should be noted in all this is the moral aspect. All these White officers were vested with functions in the Red army, privileged in various respects in comparison to the privations suffered by the rest of the population; right up to the very moment of their treachery, they pretended loyalty towards the revolutionary regime. They worked fraternally alongside the Communists. But when the fortress at Krasnaia Gorka was taken, they had some two hundred Communists and sympathisers arrested, and half of them were shot in small groups over a period of forty-eight hours. Clearly it never crossed their minds that one could do anything other than kill a Communist who had been defeated or taken prisoner. The same psychology was manifested in an order issued by General Rodzianko: 'In the name of the Constituent Assembly', it began, ' I instruct you to execute Communists.' At the same time Yudenich also imposed the death penalty on anyone who failed to hand over Communists. It is the mentality shown by the Versailles forces at the time of the Paris Commune. During the last week of May in 1871 the reactionaries killed more than thirty thousand people in eight days. In 1918 the White terror in Finland killed ten to twelve thousand insurgents, and more than seventy thousand were tortured in the prisons. White terror, which is embryonic in the current treacheries and shootings, has the particular feature that it tends to kill its victims all together and that it aims to exterminate the most vigorous and the most conscious element among its opponents. That is the main thing that distinguishes it from Red terror, which it precedes and is the cause of, and which has no other purpose than to break the resistance of a minority. Hence the latter is by far the less bloody. In this respect it is also possible to draw a comparison between the mentality of the reactionary junker, who is convinced of the divine right of the rich, and that of the idealistic rebel, who may certainly be provoked to violence, but who cannot be made into the complacent executioner who is happy to be at the service of 'order'.

22–24 JUNE 1919

The point of greatest danger has passed, although neither Yudenich's offensive nor that of the White Karelian bands have yet been halted. In the north, the British are also attacking in the direction of Lake Onega; in the south-west the Poles have inflicted losses on us and captured positions. But Petrograd has overcome its surprise, and is on its guard; at every moment it is becoming more confident. By a sort of acquired momentum, the energy devoted to defence, above all internal defence, is developing and rapidly increasing.

A decision by the central committee of the Communist party, published as early as 14 June, when militants were being sent to the front, requires all party members to learn immediately how to handle a machine-gun.

Now extraordinary precautionary measures are coming one after the other. In all this we are aware of the strong hand of the head of internal security, Peters. These measures are worth noting; born from the practice of civil war, they provide the basis for a whole theory.

First of all, it is vital to strike the class enemy, the Whites. To this end, order No 960, of 22 June, requires that every citizen must always carry with him a labour certificate issued at his place of work. All those who exploit the labour of others, or who do not work, are required to present themselves within three days at the Palace of Labour, where they will be registered and will receive special documents. The house committees and the militia responsible for the control of the streets will check that this order is being applied. This is a direct blow against the White population, made up of speculators, intellectuals who are irredeemably hostile to the soviet regime, and the old and new rich—all are doing their utmost to keep their heads down and bide their time. When they came to be registered, all those who were considered to be suspect were immediately sent to do defence work.

A *mandatory regulation* of 21 June establishes new controls based on strict rules as to the circulation of cars and motorcycles by day or by night, within or outside the city. A vehicle requires two different permits, one for moving around the town between 7.00am and 11.00pm, and one for the period between 11.00pm and 7.00am. A special permit is required for any journey outside the city. All motor vehicles, without exception, will be checked by the militia. If we recall that even the smallest counter-revolutionary attack would require a number of rapid journeys, this precaution is obviously essential.

The order to hand over immediately all weapons which have remained in the hands of citizens, and the house-to-house searches which followed this order, were aimed at disarming the enemy within. At present the task is to arm the workers. The same weapons will serve for this task!

On 24 June the Workers' Defence committee published a decree in the name of Zinoviev and Peters ordering the formation of workers' reserve regiments by the trade union organisation. They will be made up of workers from the factories of Petrograd; headquarters will be set up by district and factory.

Peters has issued a poster which reiterates that 'anyone found in possession of weapons or ammunition after 24 June will be immediately shot'. And thus we are brought back to the question of the terror, which is the logical conclusion of all these measures.

I believe that I have seen the birth of the terror during these anxious days. A list of sixty-six people who have been shot has just been published by the Special Commission. It takes up a whole column in the newspaper. Each name is followed by a brief indication of the reason for the sentence. Included are those responsible for the betrayals at Krasnaia Gorka, Kronstadt and everywhere else, and their accomplices; there are monarchists and members of the Republican Centre, people who were more or less agents of the 'Simon' espionage agency, officers and civil servants guilty of forgery, two militia men who had sold their weapons, agents of the Special Commission itself sentenced for theft or extortion, a trio of speculators—which means, in a time of famine, people responsible for starvation. The total is sixty-six. Less than the number of our people that they shot in the Krasnaia Gorka fort immediately after the betrayal. So, during this month of implacable civil war, in Petrograd, Red terror has taken a total of less than a hundred and fifty lives, if we are to believe the announcements that have been published. (And why should they not all have been published, since it is principally by means of such announcements that the terror has an effect on the enemy?) But even if we follow rumour, which always exaggerates and distorts, and double or triple this figure, then still, in this battle of the civil war, only a derisory number of Whites have fallen victim to the Reds. When they capture the smallest town, more assorted workers, 'Jews' and 'Bolsheviks' are put to death.

The other night I was at the Special Commission headquarters, perhaps at the very time when the fate of those sixty-six was being decided. Peters was there, in army uniform, following by telephone the various internal and external defence operations which were still in an indeterminate state. The news arrived, one item after another: 'A certain fort at Kronstadt is on fire. British planes are bombing the fleet. On a certain battleship treachery is being planned. At Krasnaia Gorka, the Whites are systematically shooting their prisoners and transmitting appeals to the British fleet by radio. The general staff of a certain Red regiment have been captured by Yudenich and shot. Balakhovich has burned a village. In a certain street a clandestine printing press has been discovered with manifestos in favour of the Constituent Assembly. In a certain house, a stock of guns and grenades has been found. Here there is a machine-gun in an attic. There, bombs in a cellar. An agent of the National Centre has been arrested on the Finnish frontier: he was carrying messages from the Whites in the city. In Karelia the Whites have won a victory. In X. Street, speculators and brigands have robbed the local co-operative: the population will have no sugar for the next fortnight. Somewhere else a bad Communist has committed a theft. There has just been an attack on the Moscow railway line, with the aim of cutting off food supplies.' Such are the reports which a man invested with the highest responsibility for the defence of the revolutionary capital receives from morning to evening and from evening to morning. He knows that the slightest mistake—error, hesitation or weakness—can lead to a fatal betrayal. Everywhere there are concealed hatreds. Only a small number of men can be relied on—and the mass of armed workers, heroic, but ignorant, suffering and slaves to their instincts, whom the Whites are surreptitiously trying to undermine. And now the revolutionary, at his post amid this enormous danger, is brought this list of sixty-six Whites, treacherous officers, intellectuals who support the Entente, starvers of the people, shady 'Communists'. Did he have any choice? Was not terror imposed on him by implacable necessity? Perhaps this very evening the revolution will collapse in our blood and in the blood of a whole people. The old law is: kill or be killed. But for us it is nonetheless something higher and less cruel than what has existed through the ages, for it is translated as follows: Break the past of lies, oppression, exploitation, authority, so that the future shall belong to the free workers in a free society. Crush this handful of backward-looking reactionaries—sixty-six, one hundred or three hundred, what does it matter!—in order to spare the tens of thousands of workers whom they will slaughter if they come out on top. Crush this incipient reaction at whatever cost, because if it were to triumph even for a moment it would be a calamity for the whole of humanity.

And then let those who have not lived through these hours of civil war, let those who—workers and 'revolutionaries'—are living peacefully in bourgeois servility, cast the first stone!

END OF JUNE 1919

In his office in Kronversky Prospect, furnished simply with a writingdesk overflowing with books and manuscripts and a few tall bookcases, in this austere study, its only decoration a few valuable Chinese ornaments, a Buddha and some vases, Alexis Maximovich—the first and greatest of the masters of Russian culture at the present time—Maxim Gorky,* is frowning; his

---

* Contrast the very different account of Gorky in *Memoirs of a Revolutionary*. [Translator's note]

features are apparently harder than usual and his complexion more ashen. Beneath his toothbrush moustache, you can sense that he is muttering with sadness, and beyond that, with suffering. Alexis Maximovich is the great witness of this epoch: a human consciousness who sees everything, knows everything, understands everything about the revolutionary tragedy and obstinately peers into the future. He is on the sidelines of the immediate action, but the great suffering of the civil war evokes many echoes in him. Perhaps nobody feels more devastated than he does by the sensation of terror, of dictatorship, of war, three aspects of humanity. His whole life has been that of an observer, a thinker, and, though he denies it, a sensitive person. And that is what is truly terrible: to preserve the profound sensitivity of an artist who loves humanity at a time when men are hurling themselves at each other in the trenches and in the streets. But this witness, whose speech is stern, sometimes so much so that a dark veil seems to pass in front of the clear kindly gaze of his grey eyes, this witness is on our side, the side of the Reds, with his whole heart. Because he is with the future, distant, vast, 'planetary' to use his term, the future which will eventually be born of the immense present suffering.

There was an excellent woman comrade from Hungary there. We spoke about Soviet Hungary, where a marvellous peaceful social transformation is being carried out. At its dawning, this Soviet Republic did not shed a single drop of blood. Gorky's face lit up when this was referred to. 'Yes, certainly, with great joy I will write something for Hungary! Over there, things are turning out quite differently than with us. That's Europe, over there!' And he smiled. The peaceful revolution, the new society being born almost painlessly, after the abdication of a bourgeoisie crushed under the weight of its own guilt; what a magnificent and beautiful dream! Maxim Gorky's face lit up.

The executive of the Third International seems to have less confidence in such an idyll, although to an outsider's eyes no cloud seems to darken the perspective of a Red Hungary. A message addressed to it by Zinoviev on 12 June ended with the repeated appeal: 'Take arms! Organise!—Organise! Take arms!' The future will judge as to who was right—the distrustful orator or the thinker touched by a magnificent hope.

END OF JUNE 1919

'The Red forces have just gone onto the attack outside
Petrograd. They have advanced some seven to ten miles, captured
machine-guns and artillery, taken prisoners. Hundreds of Whites
have come over to our side, most of them with their weapons.'
This despatch, dated 24 June, was signed by a member of the
Revolutionary Council of the Tenth Army, W Shatov.

Between two operations at the front, Shatov makes brief
appearances among us in Petrograd. This warm, cheerful young
man, large and burly with a round, florid face, always clean shaven,
with the calm, good-natured expression of a man who enjoys the
pleasures of life, has a special position here. He is, in short, our
'general', after having spent several months as the 'governor' of
Red Petrograd—and after having in the first months of the soviet
regime been the 'transport dictator' of the Northern Commune.
The strange thing in all this—at least in the eyes of people
accustomed to traditional judgements—is that William Shatov is
an anarchist.

Just after the October revolution, he found himself, by force
of circumstance, 'governor' of the city, since the Red Guards—
among whom there were many libertarians—constituted in fact the
only real power and they elected him unanimously. His liveliness,
his convinced optimism, his resolve, his overflowing energy have
since made him quite naturally into one of the leaders of the Red
army. One day he was asked: 'But how can you, as an anarchist,
exercise authority?' He replied with a question: 'Should we not
have defended Petrograd?'

I know what terrible experiences he has passed through.
During the questionable negotiations at Brest-Litovsk, the
German offensive made Petrograd, still the Soviet capital at this
time, more and more clearly a target; it was necessary to start the
evacuation of the huge city, in order to save its main art treasures,
its stocks of arms, ammunition, and gold, and the main
departments of the revolutionary government. But there was no
obstacle to the activity of selfish desires. In a city where three
hundred thousand Red proletarians were making sacrifices every
day, there were three times that number of bourgeois, petty
bourgeois, workers who had adopted bourgeois attitudes or who

were backward, in short, people of the old regime, steeped in its mentality and its customs, grasping, unscrupulous and lacking in revolutionary idealism, who thought only of their own personal interests and didn't mind what they did to pursue them. Out of this crowd, the majority, panic-stricken, wanted to flee Petrograd. Even before the trains arrived in the station they were besieged. Sometimes the drivers and stokers were killed; men emerged from the crowd who knew how to drive a train and got it going. On the roofs of the carriages, on the tenders, everywhere that there was room for a human being carrying a bundle or a bag, men and women piled up. On the footboards there were bitter fights for a place. Knives and revolvers pierced anonymous flesh. As the locomotive set off, it crushed those whom the general pushing and shoving had made fall beneath its wheels. Every boarding was a ferocious rush followed by scuffles. A train almost always left a trail of blood behind it. These trains had no more windows, hardly any seats or doors. The anarchist William Shatov took on the job of organising the evacuation. He took many measures and certainly his persuasive energy, which made an impact on the railway workers, was not the least important factor in his success. But he had no hesitation in lining the tracks with a row of machine-guns, and if necessary emptying several coaches under fire from Maxim guns. At this price, the evacuation was carried out and the transport system of the Northern Commune was re-established despite the famine and the foreign and civil wars. Otherwise it would have been a total disaster.

Shatov relates these things—and many others—with the energy and zest of a free man, one free even from ideological traditions and preconceptions. His great merit is that he is unable to sacrifice action to abstract ideas. For this profoundly Americanised Russian worker action comes before any theory because it is life. Anarchy is not an ideal formula; it must be life and can be born only from action. Does the revolution not need violence, authority, constraint? Is not the evil facing us at present the evil of civil war? Shatov considers it is better to win at this price than to be defeated for—and by—the ideal. Although working in complete agreement with it, he does not join the Communist party. 'Sooner or later,' he says, ' we shall find ourselves enemies again.' But if you watch him at work, it seems as if this eventuality is still quite a long way away. For him, and for a certain number of clear-sighted spirits, anarchy cannot arise today from the chaos of violence and unrestrained desires, but it must come later as the product of a new culture and a new organisation of production in communist society.

Other anarchists have criticised him bitterly. They bravely got themselves killed for the revolution in various fashions, sometimes harmful ones. In order to preserve their purity of principle, they abandoned the attempt to control events and turned down historic responsibilities.

At other times, terror has raged more severely, but it has been for the same reasons and in the same atmosphere created by permanent conspiracy within, foreign intervention, treachery, famine, and the threat of death in an infinite number of guises.

In these conditions I don't think one can fail to have recourse to terror, although the duty of every revolutionary must obviously be to limit it and to define its scope: and that, precisely, in order to make it into a more formidable weapon. For it is not by striking a great deal that you win, it is by striking in the right place.

The history of all revolutions contains similar pages. Those describing the revolution of modern times which has brought about the most profound social transformation are particularly striking, allowing us to draw a parallel between Year II of the French revolution and Year II of the Russian revolution. Emigration, intervention, counter-revolutionary coalitions, mass reactionary insurrections like that of the Vendée,* separatist movements within, permanent conspiracy, famine and terror—it cannot be pure coincidence that these features occur identically in both these great historical cases. Rather it is the fact that the course of world wars obeys general laws which science will codify later on, but which we can already glimpse at the present time. Besides, we don't need to evoke the epic of 1793 to understand that a rich and powerful class will not let itself be dispossessed without a fight to the death.

---

* Area of Western France, scene of a counter-revolutionary royalist rising 1793-96. *[Translator's note]*

This fight to the death, in Red Russia, has had many victims. At certain times these days of hatred are so painful that one feels on the brink of despair, and one loses faith in humanity, and in ideas, and in oneself. The horizon seems to block out all light. The evil madness of humanity seems so great that there is no way out. The Russian revolutionaries have all gone through such doubt and anguish. Some have given in. Most have emerged strengthened in their commitment to the ideal.

For the essential thing is that during the days when the nightmare hovered above the Red city, thousands and thousands of people lived there—and were prepared to get themselves killed—supported by the awareness that they were carrying out a vast, necessary and noble task, that they were working for the future and for the whole of humanity.

Two or three ideas, but lofty, radiant ideas, stuck obstinately in their brains: the principle of the commune, the fraternity of workers, the International, fraternity between races. And they applied themselves to the liberation of women, to ensuring the security and well-being of children, to ceaselessly and fiercely cleansing their own ranks.

The essential thing is that, in those barbarous days, the Red city in arms guarded like a treasure its libraries, its schools, its palaces transformed into people's clubs or children's homes, its poets, its scholars, its actors, its musicians; that the love of culture was strong enough to bring together, under the threat of the British guns, on the very day when great betrayals took place, noble crowds around the composer Glazunov—or around young women reading the humble epic of *The Twelve*, who are in mystic fashion in the noble and lucid poem of Alexander Blok the twelve apostles of the new Gospel.

The essential thing is that, after having approached it and seen it at work, one can admire this suffering and passionate humanity of revolutionaries, sacrificed, often in what is best and most sacred about it, to the future. The essential thing is that we know well that the very blood shed in these struggles is fertile: for our job is to ensure a little more well-being, justice and enlightenment here below, in the new society.

PETROGRAD, 1-7 JANUARY 1920

The endangered city

Petrograd: *Year two of the revolution*

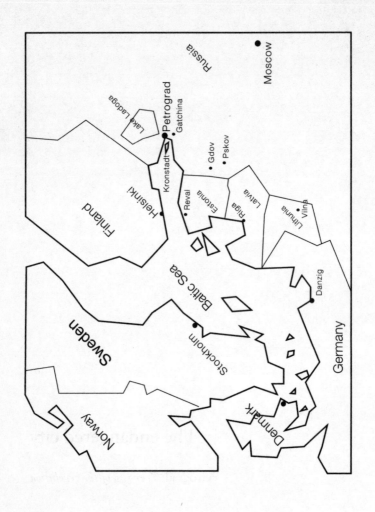

WITH AFFECTION AND RESPECT, I dedicate this testimony to the memory of my brothers and comrades:

V-O Lichtenstadt (Mazin)
Max Flinberg
John Reed
Raymond Lefebvre
Lepetit
Marcel Vergeat
Sasha Tubin

who, having come from all parts of the world and all points on the intellectual spectrum, died for the revolution. For they knew that in the century of the dollar and of mustard gas, life is only worth living if it is devoted to the one great cause: that of the proletariat.

My road to Russia

These notes on life inside Petrograd in October 1919, that is, at a particularly heroic and important stage of its revolutionary destiny, were written by a 'foreigner'.

Although the author is of Russian origin, he was born in Belgium and had only just arrived in Russia. His first contact with Russia and with the realities of the revolution had come in late January, 1919. Prior to that he had been active for twelve years in the anarchist movements of Belgium, France and Spain. From the time of the October revolution, he thought of himself as a Communist; he joined the Russian Communist party in May 1919. Thus his observations and reflections are those of a Communist formed in the libertarian traditions of the Latin countries. He set them down having constantly in mind his former comrades; his concern was to counter their objections, in the hope of enabling them to understand better the proletarian revolution; he also felt the need of a constant dialogue with himself.

Before the founding of the parties of the Third International there were not, in reality, any revolutionary Marxist parties in the Latin countries. At best you could locate the embryos of such parties in the intransigent tendencies within the Socialist Parties, especially in Guesdism in France, which had its moments of splendid revolutionary steadfastness, and even began to create, in northeastern France, a mass workers' movement. But as a general rule parliamentary opportunism dominated in the Socialist Parties; and as a natural reaction, the revolutionary elements moved away from these parties, seeking different roads. In France the socialism of Jaurès blossomed, very eloquent, but so moderate, so pink, so permeated with the ideals of bourgeois democracy; meanwhile almost all the revolutionary forces of the French proletariat turned towards syndicalism, enthused by the new ideas of direct action and the general strike. Within the syndicalist movement or outside it, the anarchists still laid claim to a higher revolutionary purity, seeking to react against the bureaucratisation of the unions. And it must be said that most of the time, with the best intentions in the world, all their dedication and even heroism succeeded only in multiplying sects and sub-sects, ludicrous or tragic deviations (advocacy of Esperanto, vegetarianism, nudism and the cult of free love everywhere; banditry in France; terrorism in Spain).

So, for the revolutionary workers of Western Europe, the October revolution was a spectacular revelation. It gave them more than an example to follow, more than a boundless source of hope; it gave them a body of doctrine, methods of struggle, an education; it gave them leaders. From 1917 on there were many of us in the Latin countries who recognised all this, albeit in a confused fashion. We were looking for our road towards the Russian revolution, from which we were separated by many miles and by frontiers bristling with cannon—and perhaps even more by the pernicious traditions of reformist socialism and the childish illusions of anarchism which had grown up in reaction to it.

So my journey towards Communism lasted some 12 years.
My journey towards *the endangered city* lasted 17 months.
On 5 January 1919, as evening fell, some twenty of us, surrounded by police, left the concentration camp at Précigné in France. Freezing cold and thin from hunger, dressed in old threadbare clothes, we went out joyfully into the cold night. We were twenty 'Bolsheviks' who had been interned for many months and who were now to be exchanged with the Soviet government for officers from the French military mission in Moscow who had

been held prisoner until now.

I had left Spain on my way to Russia at the end of July 1917, when the preparations for insurrection in Barcelona were ending up in failure;[1] the French authorities had held me prisoner for fifteen months in various concentration camps. We were kept there within a triple enclosure—guns, barbed wire and walls; the soldiers, to whom we were presented as a gang of enemy agents, constantly pointed their guns at us. Our numbers were reduced by epidemics; we heard nothing of the Russian revolution apart from the daily dose of mad slanders served up by the bourgeois press. As a result we—the whole group of comrades of Russian origin, both syndicalists and anarchists—felt every day more closely bound to the Red October, every day more communist. On the first anniversary of the victory of October 1917, we were perhaps the only people in France to celebrate it quite openly, under the astonished eyes of our gaolers, in a monastery courtyard that had been turned into a prison.

What a wave of enthusiasm was aroused at that time among the working masses by the mere thought of the Russian revolution! Cloistered behind prison walls, we only got an inkling of it from occasional clandestine letters. We were suddenly made fully aware of it as we were leaving France, in a small town on the Channel coast, where we arrived after nightfall.

Abbeville. The little town had been shelled; some roofs had been blown off, the windows were darkened and the streets unlit. Accompanied by plain-clothes police we went to a little restaurant to get some nourishment for our poor comrade Barakov, a sailor suffering from tuberculosis who was returning to Russia to die on the soil of the revolution; his health had been destroyed—because of his refusal of discipline as an active trade unionist—in the prison cells of the great American ships. The tiny room was full of British soldiers, and thick clouds of pipe-smoke rose up towards the paraffin lamps. Our group of pale people surrounding a sick man, and watched over by two gentlemen of such a special demeanour, attracted their attention.

'Who are you?'

'Bolsheviks. Prisoners. On our way to Russia...'

I shall never forget the impact this revelation made. We were immediately surrounded by an excited group of men; every face was that of a friend, hands were stretched out to shake ours, we were offered wine and cigarettes, and emotional voices declared: 'So are we! So are we! We're part of it too! You'll see later on!' They went to fetch their mates from the other cafés nearby; these embittered, battered soldiers didn't know what to do to convince us that that they were on our side with all their workers' hearts. What they said was quite true. At this very time serious mutinies were taking place in the British army not far from Calais.

Fifteen days at sea brought us from Dunkirk to Finland. On board ship, treated with great care, we were guarded by Senegalese soldiers. In their helmets, their greatcoats covered with sheepskin, their heavy peasant hands gripping their bayonets, they seemed to be the most silent, the hardest, the most unconscious of gaolers. But when they were alone with one of us on the empty deck, they sometimes gave us broad smiles.

I reached Petrograd one day in February. The first time that I visited some distant relatives, I found myself in the presence of an old lady with a *pince-nez* and angular features, who spoke in a very low voice and a conspiratorial, wailing manner. When she found out I had come from France, she displayed excessive delight. 'My goodness!' she muttered, 'how lucky you are! You were still in France, twenty days ago!' Then she began to question me eagerly:

'Tell me! Won't the British come and rescue us from the *Bolsheviks?*...Aren't the French getting ready?...They say the Romanians?...Why is Finland afraid?' When she heard me reply that nobody would come, the old lady with the *pince-nez* began to cry. It was my first contact with the *obyvatelschina*² of the civil war. Ever since then I have imagined it with the symbolic features of that tearful old petty bourgeois woman, living in fear and anticipation: in fear of the new life clearly and harshly proclaimed by the proletarian revolution, in the insane anticipation of interventions by providence which were now impossible. Throughout the civil war we constantly found ourselves up against this *obyvatelschina*, a petty bourgeoisie steeped in hatred, powerless, hopelessly mediocre.

It was Year Two. Other years, since the two assaults of the Whites on Petrograd, the second of which seemed for a while to be on the point of succeeding—have brought us other sorrows and other victories. But it seems to me more and more that every memory of that year and of those battles should be preserved. Such is the justification for these observations and reflections from an observer who had come from afar.

Second attack by General Yudenich's White army on Petrograd, 23-30 October 1919

Perpetual danger facing Petrograd

Is the city of the revolution not permanently in danger?

As a result of its geographical situation, Red Petrograd lives under the permanent threat of an attack. It is an object of fear—and sometimes of envy—to Finland, which is scarcely thirty miles away with no natural obstacles in between. It is blockaded by a British naval squadron, whose guns have been trained on Kronstadt for months. It is attacked or threatened by the White army of some counter-revolutionary pseudo-government which has taken refuge in Tallinn; it is attacked or threatened by the Estonian army. It has faced so many direct threats!

The Kaiser's armies threatened it, when they had taken Riga and were continuing their offensive northwards. After the February revolution, Kornilov, aspiring to military dictatorship, marched on Petrograd, which was saved by its revolutionary enthusiasm. After the October revolution, Kerensky, surrounded at Gatchina by cadets from the military colleges and a few loyal battalions, wanted to try an attack on the capital. The Bolshevik Red Guards broke his offensive at Pulkovo. And how many times since then has Mannerheim's Finland seemed to be on the brink of opening hostilities? In Helsinki people were making commercial deals about real estate in Petrograd. Then the Estonian White army's successive offensives were unleashed, each beginning with a victory (the first time, capture of Narva; the second time, capture of Yamburg; and this time, capture of Yamburg, Gatchina and Krasnoe Selo, that is, of districts immediately adjoining the capital).

Petrograd is a front-line city. The air you breathe there is more vibrant than elsewhere. You can feel the nervous tension and the awakening of a crowd living on permanent alert.

But since it has lived through so many crises and critical periods, the Red City has become used to not easily getting upset about the dangers it is threatened with. It has acquired a sort of confidence in its good fortune.

People cannot conceive that it could fall, be captured, defeated, crushed underfoot by outsiders. And we can be sure that they are not mistaken. The causes which have thus far made it unyielding are continuing to protect it.

Its enemies are divided by profound hatreds and irreconcilable conflicts of interest; they loathe each other. Its defenders are aware of the historic greatness of their task. Petrograd, a revolutionary capital and an intellectual capital; Petrograd where the whole history of a social war lasting fifty years is written on the stones of the buildings and on the pavements of the streets; Petrograd, gateway to a vast Russia open to the seas of northern Europe, remains one of the centres of the revolution. 'The republic', says Trotsky, 'has three trump cards which it must not lose in any circumstances: Petrograd, Moscow, Tula.' What splendid things are at stake in these battles!

The rout

Since the last alert (mid-June 1919), what is called normal life had resumed its course. The theatres were packed with people every night, concerts, lectures and meetings brought their usual audiences together; even trade was 'picking up'. In fact a large number of shops had opened.

Jewellers, antique dealers, perfume sellers, traders in luxury items, booksellers, grocers—in whose shops, alas!, you find nothing but drinks and substitutes for coffee—and assorted speculators were doing excellent business. Trade in the markets, swarming with motley crowds, was in full swing.

Familiarity with an undefined, distant danger, which was considered fatalistically, allowed life to follow its normal course and people scarcely got excited when among the reports from the front the newspapers published three short lines announcing that 'under pressure from superior enemy forces our troops have abandoned their positions at Yamburg'—though this is a position of crucial importance, since, 72 miles from Petrograd, opposite Narva, it is the Red city's only defensive advanced post. Once Yamburg was lost, the Red army could rely only on Krasnoe Selo and Gatchina.

Isn't official information wonderful! The news had been known by almost the entire population for nearly two days. And it is a noteworthy phenomenon how quickly news—even when kept secret—spreads through the crowds.

What had happened? Well-informed people, party members, working with the executive committee of the soviet, were not surprised. 'Our troops have had enough. Pretty badly fed, inadequately clothed, kept at the front without being replaced for weeks and months, they are also demoralised amid the inactivity of the Estonian front. A few tanks (five) were sent against them and it was panic flight, rout, every man for himself'. While a female comrade was saying this to me in the tram taking us to Smolny, explaining in such simple terms *that there is no relief* because there are no trained combat units, and that at 'the very word tank panic spreads through the ranks,' I remembered a humble soldier, my companion during a hard night's work, and I understood.

The soldier's mentality

He had come with me one night when we were making house-to-house searches. We were tired and depressed by the job we had to do; we stopped outside the locked doors of houses, where sometimes we had to hammer with rifle-butts. Then as the reddish candlelight made enormous shadows dance around us, giving a strange illumination from below to his rough peasant face, we exchanged a few words. He was cold; his gun pressed against his chest, he rubbed his hands vigorously and said to me:

'I shall soon have done eight years...When the war started, I had nearly finished my period of service. I fought in Bukovina, in Galicia, outside Riga. Then we thought there would be peace at last, but the civil war started up.'

He wasn't blaming anyone. He summed up the causes briefly:

'Ah! The Entente, the Allies!'

And he didn't find any better way of expressing his feelings than a vague insult, almost muttered, directed at those who, surrounded by comfort and honours on the other side of Europe, were deciding on the killing to take place over here:

'Scum!'

No. I'm not surprised they sometimes run away, terrified by a tank or about to drop with terrible weariness, our poor grey troop of soldiers, whose blood has been shed every day for so many years.

I didn't know what to say to that particular soldier, for words seemed so empty and worthless in the face of reality. The old regime had robbed this man, like all his fellows, of three years of life; the old world, committing its great crime, had turned him for four years into a thing that kills, a being that is killed. The revolution promised so much to him, it suffered and struggled for his sake, but what has it done for him?

He is doing virtually the same job as before. He is still trapped in the infernal cycle of war, my brother the soldier, and perhaps—what a terrible thought!—he doesn't understand the reason for this one any better than for the other. The trenches, the lice, the wounds, the shrapnel, the buildings that are captured, the buildings that are lost, the comrades who fall; that is what it still is, what it always is for him!

Now this man has not become a *soldier*. He has remained a worker of the land. His land, his *isba* (log hut), his wife are waiting for him somewhere, and that is where his life is.

So sometimes he has moments of weakness. His head spins, he doesn't know where truth and justice are, where are the enemy—those who want his eternal enslavement—or where are his friends.

There is a terrible irony in this fact: the revolution has been fighting on five fronts, for two years, because it proclaimed that the worker must no longer fight against his brother—and that all men of goodwill are brothers in labour; this irony and this profound injustice perturb him.

Alone, in a group, or in whole companies, he 'goes over to the enemy', that is, he flees towards the enemy, with the crazy hope that this will be the end. But over there, he is mobilised afresh, this time to fight for the rich, under the disdainful eye of

generals who know how to train *muzhiks* for obedience. He
crosses the front line again in the opposite direction, he comes
back to us and fights stoically, he who doesn't want to fight at all.

The Versailles* troops have forced a door open

The fact remains that this time the shock is terrible. In
twenty-four hours the atmosphere of the city has been
transformed. From tranquillity and indifference we have gone
over to the nervous tension that is felt on the eve of battle. On
Thursday 23 October, *Pravda* publishes the declaration of martial
law, with a series of draconian measures: closing of theatres and
cinemas; ban on going out after 8.00 p.m. without a special
permit; closing of shops and markets. This last measure seems to
be a mistake, and I see no reason for it. The communal shops have
so few goods that it is impossible not to turn to the market and the
trade in secret contraband.

The same day, prices double: for the order having been
given, it doesn't actually stop anything, but in an irritating fashion
makes things more complicated. Who gave the order? Why? No
checking mechanism is functioning. No mechanism for criticism
exists at this time of total implacable dictatorship. And certainly if
I am right in thinking it is a mistake, it is a serious one, because it
immediately antagonises two thirds of the population by making it
even more difficult to obtain food supplies. All it needed was a
badly drafted, ill-conceived order, the ill will or whim of
somebody, somewhere in an improvised general staff. For the
combat apparatus of the general staff of internal defence is being
feverishly improvised. The enemy is less than twenty-five miles
away, and in several places our troops are fleeing in panic: the fate
of Red Petrograd will be at stake in a final battle which may end
up being fought in our own streets. The Versailles troops have
forced a door open.

The next day, 24 October, the situation is worse. Krasnoe
Selo, Gatchina, Pavlovsk, Dietskoe Selo (formerly Tsarskoe³) have
been occupied by the White army. It has only one more stage to

---

* Counter-revolutionary troops from Versailles crushed the Paris
Commune of 1871. *[Translator's note]*

complete. Never has the danger been so great. The whole working-class population up to the age of forty-five has been mobilised.

At Smolny the broad corridors are filled with a mass of armed people who are being rapidly equipped. They are factory workers, in overcoats, in *touloups* (sheepskin coats): they are fitting cartridge-belts on their civilian clothes and taking rifles, which gives them the appearance of being rebels.

The Communist party has mobilised all its members, men and women. The women are also going to the front, in contingents of fighters or of stretcher bearers. A decision of the central committee is sending immediately to the front those militants who hold 'positions of trust'.

But the city still looks normal. You can just about distinguish additional activity in the great thoroughfares where motorcycles, cars and lorries from the army or the internal defence forces are moving in all directions.

The newspapers say that Trotsky is coming. He has not been here for a long time. The situation here must be considered very serious for him to leave Moscow at a time when things are going rather badly on the Southern front. General Denikin's army has taken Kursk and Orel, two cities in Greater Russia, which had never been occupied since the revolution. He is threatening Tula, the arsenal of the Red army, and Moscow. People shake their heads. On the trams and in the streets you can pick up significant scraps of conversation. Clearly the majority of the population, those who are not workers or Communists and who have no revolutionary education, all those who have no interest in maintaining the new regime, are awaiting events without confidence; and many think it is the beginning of the end. You would think so if you observed the fatal apathy of all these passers-by who are getting on with their usual activities, in a manner showing no concern about events that are too immediate, while perhaps tomorrow the Petrograd Commune will shed its blood on the barricades.

It is a grey, damp day; a wearisome drizzle is falling.

There was a time...

I know. There was a time when everything seemed lost.
Everything? No. Petrograd. But for me, for thousands of others,
now, Petrograd is everything. Its fall would be something
inconceivable, like the first stage of the collapse of the revolution.

The humming telephone wires that linked Smolny to the
Kremlin carried grave voices and grave words. Lenin. Zinoviev. In
both places attentive brains were striving to assess the balance of
forces, and to weigh up the chances, which seemed very slight.
These men could see closing around the frontiers of the former
sixteenth-century Grand-Duchy of Muscovy the circle of death of
the counter-revolution. Paris Commune, 1905 in Russia, Finland.
The proletariat seemed to be advancing only from one defeat to
another, and they knew it. Would 1919 be an ill-omened date?
How could we resist everywhere? Could we avoid sacrificing
Petrograd? At a certain moment there were grave doubts. They
say that even Lenin was convinced. Zinoviev wanted to stand firm.
But Trotsky's train was making its way to the endangered city.

My friend M. saw Lenin during these days. Vladimir Ilyich
had his usual calm, solid forehead, his usual brisk laugh, jovial and
sarcastic: 'Well, what about it?' he said, with a triumphant burst of
laughter. 'We'll go back to underground activity'.

Two trains packed with our people's children, whom the
executioners would not spare despite the courage of their parents,
have set off for Volga, Perm, Ekaterinburg, Votkinsk. Comrades
are preparing to remain behind if Petrograd falls, to begin illegal
work straightaway. They are equipping themselves with passports
from the old regime. Others are studying the map, making vague
plans, wondering whether, if the battle in the streets goes badly, it
is possible to cross the Neva, whether...a risky retreat, on foot,
without supplies, along the river, without being quite sure where
they would be going to.

An article by Trotsky

This evening *Izvestia* publishes a leading article by Trotsky:
Petrograd is also defending itself from within. Two columns of cold
logical argument, terribly logical and clear.

As I read it, I remember his metallic voice, his regular

gestures, his imposing military appearance which is deliberately very simple, his concentrated energy, sure of itself, imperturbable, emanating from his whole being. Nobody but he could write this article, write it as it is, simple, hard and firm.

From the military point of view, he explains, the most advantageous course of action at the present time would be to draw the enemy into the city and fight them there. Since the telephone and telegraphic systems are in our hands, and the strategic points are fortified and defended with the support of the working population, Petrograd, with its maze-like streets, its canals, its houses turned into fortresses or concealing ambushes, would be a death-trap for the small White army. There are indeed a few lines where he writes of saving artistic treasures and innocent victims (whose blood would not be on our hands in any case), but the conclusion is unambiguous. If the regular army cannot carry out its task, Petrograd will have to defend itself within its own walls. 'Be prepared, Petrograd! Perhaps you are destined in these October days to write the most glorious page of your history!'

When an army leader writes that, the fearful inhabitant, accustomed to the obligatory optimism of the authorities, expects the worst. This evening the atmosphere is heavy with anxiety. I have just read this article from *Izvestia*, pasted up on Nevsky Prospect.

A whole silent group of people has formed in front of the poster. Suddenly we jump: somewhere, behind the Gostinny Dvor, on the other side of the roadway, a bomb has apparently just gone off. But it is only a purely nervous reaction which doesn't bother anyone. Evening is falling, grey and gloomy with rain.

Among the citizens conversations betray a beginning of panic. It is said that planes have just bombed Smolny; they say a bomb has destroyed a house in the Sadovaia. There's no truth in it. Where do these rumours come from? They are born unconsciously from fear, or from the overexcitement of people's imaginations; and they spread from one conversation to the next, unconsciously inflated and distorted.

The organisation of internal defence has sprung up

instantaneously. To create it, it was merely necessary to use the framework of the Communist party, to mobilise cadres and members, something which was done within a few hours. Thanks to the accurate registration of forces, to the centralisation of initiatives, to the establishment of a precise correspondence between the machinery of the party and that of the government, all the energies of the city are diverted from their habitual activities to concentrate on one single task: the preparation for fighting within the city, which will be defended street by street, house by house. Attached to the party committee in each sector or administrative district of the city *troikas* are formed, committees of three, possessed of full powers to defend the sector. The president of the *troika* is the military leader of the sector. In the party premises, activity is intensifying in feverish fashion; but now, strangely, you scarcely hear the usual rattle of typewriters.

Petrograd by night

At eight o'clock, the streets are dead. But there are many patrols, guardhouses, observation posts. The internal defence has been well organised. On the corners of the streets, in pairs or in threes, militia men and women are tirelessly checking the special passes which allow people to be on the streets after the time of the curfew. Then there are patrols of soldiers, with grim childlike faces under their white *papakhas* (fur hats).

In twos and threes the Communists are also patrolling, checking on those responsible for maintaining order. They are mainly women, workers from factories and offices.

There is a roar of motorcycles. The sudden glow of an acetylene lamp dazzles me for a second. The motorbike has stopped at the edge of the pavement; it is carrying two men dressed in black leather, armed with long Mauser pistols, hanging from their belts in wooden holsters. One of them must be the head of the internal security service, for he rapidly questions the militiamen.

What is the good of this excess of precautions? It seems to me unnecessary in the absolute still of the night. There is no glimmer of light at the windows of the great stone houses, very black, very tall. There is nobody on the streets, except for party

comrades coming off duty or on their way to it. There are
thousands and thousands of us, armed, organised to defend the
revolution. We feel that we are the living force, the only force. Is
it possible that, in this dark, silent, dead city, the enemy is also
watching us?

The Communists

3.00 am, 4.00 am. The air trembles as cannon-fire
approaches. A brief detonation has made all those who are
sleeping in their dark homes, under threat, shiver. Ah! They heave
a sigh of relief. For expectation was oppressive. Now the die is
cast. It will be battle, blood on the pavements, barricades, the
Commune standing up to fight, and those who want to kill it will
pay a heavy price.

The cannon thunders, very near, very near, with great
explosions coming at intervals of a few minutes. The glass in the
windows quivers. It sounds like the breath of powerful steel
monsters. I lean out of the window. At each detonation, there are
great white flashes of lightning against the dark sky, over there
towards the harbour. Doubtless our fleet is firing. So the enemy is
approaching, perhaps already at the gates of Narva, or in the
Peterhof district. So there is fighting in the city!

The evening before last, before the great danger had been
made public, a comrade, a well-known member of the soviet, came
to see us and together we envisaged these terrible moments. Now
as I walk rapidly through the silent streets, towards the flashes and
the roar of the cannon, I can see him again, restless and excitable,
his movements rather jerky, with his fine dishevelled mane of hair
and his small, dark eyes, tired and drawn but penetrating, a man
whom underground struggle, jail and penal servitude, insurrection
and power have marked profoundly. He is a man who passionately
loves books, jewellery, statuettes, medallions—his house is full of
them. I had the distinct impression that at the very thought of
losing his collections and his books a shiver of despair ran through
his flesh and his soul.

Agitatedly, with a false laugh, he said to me: 'Oh well! We'll
abandon our books and take up guns'; then, getting more and
more excited, with feverish movements: 'If we have to surrender

Red Petrograd to them, I propose we set fire to it, that we blow it up, that we reduce it to a heap of stones! Cut the water mains, blow up bridges and power stations, defend every district, every house, stone by stone! We shall be killed to the last person, but we shall let the world know what it costs to overcome us!' And the thought of the 'neutral' and the 'innocent' scarcely affected us. Nobody is neutral any more. Those who remain silent are with the past, against the future.

At the party committee in one of the sectors of the city. It is just opposite the Marinsky theatre, in a little single-storeyed hotel where all the windows are lit up. As I approach, a strange silhouette rises up before me. A soft felt hat, an overcoat with the collar turned up, wearing a tight cartridge-belt; above the shoulder is a bayonet. The man approaches, the glass in his *pince-nez* glitters. I recognise N. a great reader and a great scribbler in the eyes of God, a peculiar character and an obstinate rebel; he is Polish or Finnish, knowing eight languages, a theologian, a legal writer, a man of letters, an anarchist, a Marxist, and God knows what else besides? We greet each other. I notice a thick book in his overcoat pocket, beneath the butt of his rifle.

'What are you reading?'

'Poincaré, *The Value of Science.*'

'Oh yes! *The Value of Science.*'

In the cellars of the committee premises, I glimpse men, fully dressed, fully armed, with their boots on, ready to leap into action at a moment's notice. I look at them for a moment, these men of the Commune now sleeping, so tired that the thought of the coming hour does not suffice to keep them awake. The sentry watching at their door looks me up and down in a stern fashion, and is only satisfied when I have shown him my party member's pass. The mysterious omnipresence of the enemy is thus manifested in the slightest movements.

The men are at their combat posts or resting; it is the women who are doing night duty, making telephone connections, ready for any job. There are about twenty of them here, in these vast rooms full of the smell of extinguished cigarettes, of leather, of ink. There are guns in a corner. There are heaps of files, papers on all the tables, cards, revolvers, little boxes of cartridges. Rolled up in their coats, young women are sleeping on a divan.

Two others are talking softly while going through a packet of letters confiscated somewhere. One is quite young, with a fresh complexion and rings round her eyes showing terrible tiredness. She is our secretary: she must be getting hardly any sleep these days. The cannon which thunders ceaselessly makes her smile. Last year, during a similar night of battle, at Pskov, she tells me, she gave birth to her first-born.

The cannon we can hear is our own. An hour ago the situation was tragic, but now things are going better.

VR Menzhinskaya, a collaborator of Lunacharsky at the Commissariat of Enlightenment, is on the telephone. She raises her face, with its regular but delicate features surrounded by a halo of white hair, towards me and tells me that a counter-attack by the officer cadets (*Kursanty*) has just recaptured Serguiero, near Peterhof. Two hours earlier a telephone message from Smolny had conveyed to all the committees the order to make final preparations for battle as quickly as possible, since the enemy might break into the city at any moment. The military command of the armed city has left Ligovo, and is occupying the Baltic Station. Here a small woman in a fur coat is carefully examining a Browning pistol. She turns round. I recognise the keen eyes of Lilina, commissar for social planning.

I think I should not be in any way surprised if I saw entering this room, wearing a red bonnet and armed with the pike of the most plebeian sections of the Commune, some *sans-culotte* friend of Hébert or Jacques Roux.* Am I not in the Jacobin Club? It is the time of the terror and the war in the Vendée; the British are fighting a war to the death against us.

Attitude of the neutral population

The cannon is still thundering. As I return, I pass not far from a group of people who are talking in a doorway. Doubtless they are tenants 'on guard' at the doors of two neighbouring

---

* Jacques-René Hébert (1757-94), revolutionary journalist, editor of *Le Père Duchesne;* Jacques Roux (1752-94), revolutionary priest, leading *enragé. [Translator's note]*

houses. A soldier, with his cheek bandaged, a woman wearing a coloured handkerchief, a *dvornik* (concierge), and someone else. They are talking of the ongoing battle, not knowing whether the cannon they can hear is ours or the enemy's. I come closer, in a state of excitement, and say: 'That's our fire you can hear...the news is excellent.'

My words are met with a hostile silence. Then the soldier with the bandaged cheek replies with a scarcely concealed snigger:

'Good Lord, the news is excellent, no doubt about it!'

Are the inhabitants against us then?

The Communists have flocked to enlist and have left for the front: but at most they are twelve or fifteen thousand in a city which still numbers more than eight hundred thousand inhabitants. The whole of the working-class population seems to have responded to the appeal with goodwill. The workers grumble too, but they still take part, for they all know very well, by instinct, that they and their cause are at stake. From Schlüsselburg practically the entire able-bodied male population has come to our assistance. But how about the inhabitants? How about the grey mass of those thousands of people who are neither workers, nor rich, nor poor, nor revolutionaries, nor absolutely ignorant, nor properly educated—the mass of those who live in a capital where so many live on small profits, hold subordinate positions, live on trade and industry; people whom the revolution has suddenly deprived of their justification for existing as well as of their means of living?

They are against communism; that I have known for a long time. In their eyes it is utopian, absurd and arbitrary, and they condemn it unequivocally. And their universal ill will is not the least cause of our difficulties. But do they want to see the victory of the Whites?

I've listened to them, I've asked them. No. They would like a change, the end of the Bolshevism that they detest, but not the old order, not a new White terror. However, they do believe in Yudenich's victory as something very probable. An intellectual, an engineer, explained to me his way of thinking:

'Within twenty-four hours the Whites can be here without encountering any serious resistance. There will be no fighting in the city. Half of the Communists have only become members out of self-interest. They will run away. There will only be a few pockets of isolated resistance. Petrograd is a ripe fruit which will fall of its own accord into the hand which is waiting to pick it. The population will blindly applaud anyone who gives them white bread.'

At first sight, these things said in a realistic tone carry a great deal of weight. In fact, they only explain the mistake made by these intellectuals, teachers, engineers, businessmen who, as we have since learned, were at this very moment organising the provisional White government for Petrograd—and who were to be shot less than a month later!

Like almost all arguments which are too realistic, this one is wrong. It is the argument of people who, lacking conviction and faith, cannot conceive of the power of a class which has achieved consciousness, and cannot understand that History is irreversible, that one cannot go against the stream, that the new principles have real force.

The apathetic and hostile inhabitants, even if ten times more numerous than the Communist proletariat, scarcely count because they represent the past, for they have no ideal. We—the Reds—despite hunger, mistakes, and even crimes—we are on our way to the city of the future.

Chaos, improvisation, doubt, anxiety

I have this great confidence. Nonetheless, when I think of the immediate danger, I feel somewhat shaken. Too much difficult or defective improvisation, too much disorder ends up by giving me a sense of impending rout. The liaison and information mechanisms are in a deplorable condition. The newspapers publish communiqués only twelve hours after rumours have circulated among the public; moreover, there are a mass of things they don't say and those are precisely the most important ones, those which would enable us to estimate the extent of the danger.

In what could be called the 'leading circles' around the executive committee of the soviet and the party committees, almost nothing is known. An appalling day!

The next morning when I arrive at the local headquarters—

which in Gogol Street occupies a large grey-stone house, formerly the property of an insurance company—I find the pavement cluttered up with furniture, bundles of paper, and packets. Typists, messengers and orderlies are hurrying through the corridors, lugging about pieces of furniture and packages. Lorries are starting up with a great noise of motors, amid clouds of suffocating smoke. The headquarters is being moved. It is going to be installed at the Peter-Paul Fortress; it will certainly be more secure in the Tsar's old citadel.

By chance I meet on a staircase the engineer Krasin. Tall, wearing a grey suit, detachable collar and cuffs, he is dressed respectably, smartly even. His face shows signs of age, with jagged features which were once handsome, and a solemn gaze; he looks like a businessman from Paris or London. What is known? I ask questions at random. Nobody knows anything about what happened during the night. The liaison centre is already at the Peter-Paul Fortress.

But there the confusion of removal is even crazier. To find a particular section of the headquarters you have to run through all the buildings which are separated by broad paths, fortifications and courtyards planted with trees. The rooms are full of furniture piled up in complete confusion. Temporary notices in blue pencil on writing paper indicate: automobile department, office of the local commander, and other departments. But the one which centralises information and draws up communiqués has got lost.

Nothing more is known at Smolny, where, since I've just come from the headquarters, I am keenly questioned. Nobody knows anything definite—except doubtless the defence headquarters. That is the reality.

This morning's *Krasnaya Gazeta* publishes the news that we have recaptured Gatchina during the night. I am confidentially informed that our troops are also once more occupying Tsarkoe Selo. At three o'clock I discover that none of this is true. The cannon can be heard intermittently. Yudenich is still at Gatchina.

The republic in danger

Yudenich is at Gatchina. Denikin, supplied by the Entente, is now treading the soil of Greater Russia. He has just advanced beyond Orel.

Orel is an old Russian city which no previous enemy had reached. From here on, right up to Tula and Moscow, there is no natural obstacle enabling serious resistance. This victorious offensive by the counter-revolution has, in less than two months, robbed us of the Crimea and the Ukraine. What forces can halt it? Trotsky was wrong, for the first time.

Our defensive struggle in Siberia is suffering the effects. I presume we have had to remove the best contingents from the troops on the Eastern front to send them into action on the Southern front. Will they get there in time?

Admiral Kolchak, who had been defeated in the Urals, is recovering as he feels us getting weaker. He has just driven us out of Tobolsk. Such is today's news. Yudenich at Gatchina, Denikin at Orel, Kolchak at Tobolsk. The assault against the Russian Commune has been launched. For anyone who is aware of the extent of the hunger and the immense weariness of the masses, the danger appears to be enormous. Since the days of Brest-Litovsk, socialist Russia has not known a threat comparable to that of the present moment.

The impression overwhelms you. The ill-starred inevitability of events, danger everywhere, war, turning on every front to our disadvantage, and here, in the expectation of street fighting, disorganisation, improvisation, lack of co-ordination, all the little mistakes, all the instances of neglect and inertia preparing perhaps for a terrible disaster.

Certainly we can fight in the streets. But with enough bread for one day or two *at the maximum*, with no food supplies for the citizens, with virtually no electricity, what would this struggle be like?

Prices of foodstuffs have leapt up. I note: flour, 300 roubles a pound (of 400 grammes); bread, 90 to 120 roubles a pound; potatoes, from 60 to 90 roubles; a dozen eggs cost 600 roubles today.

The soviet

Two and now three nights of alarms have gone by. We have got used to the imminence of danger. We have worked feverishly to prepare the defences of the city which is bristling with fortifications. This Sunday (26 October),* it has not taken on its usual Sunday appearance, bleak and stern. The trams are operating, people are in a hurry, large groups of soldiers are going up and down the Sadovaia and the Nevsky Prospect. Trotsky and Zinoviev will speak to the soviet this afternoon, about the military situation.

The hall of the Tauride Palace—where so many crowds have thronged, where so many tragic words and tragic thoughts have sprung into life—seems to be misty. From the glazed roof a mournful autumnal light comes down, dull and colourless. The main hall with its red desks, its Doric columns, the sober ornamentation in Doric style coloured in yellow shades, even the crowd of workers' delegates and Red soldiers—everything is drowned in a greyish atmosphere.

The two speakers have arrived, and have received subdued applause. Zinoviev, weighty, solemn, tired and pale with his shaven face and curly hair. Trotsky, tall and slender, upright, still giving the same impression of tense strength, with his high forehead.

Zinoviev gives an account of the military situation in the approaches to the city. We have superiority in numbers and arms. But we are facing hardened enemy units, bold, well-trained, and led by former officers who know the terrain thoroughly. They may—this possibility is in no way ruled out in our forecasts, and that is stressed—succeed in forcing entry into the city. But in no circumstances will they be able to remain there in opposition to us. Zinoviev bitterly blames the railway workers for not having done everything in their power to facilitate the movements of troops and food supplies.

After he has spoken, Trotsky examines the situation of the republic in its totality. He scarcely develops an argument, merely

---

* Serge writes 28 October, but that was a Tuesday in 1919.

[Translator's note]

cites facts from which he deduces consequences. He declares that there will soon be a reversal of the situation on the southern front. Here we shall undoubtedly be victorious. But let Petrograd be ready for everything!

There is no empty rhetoric in these speeches which are addressed, via the soviet, to the working population. Of course they are 'official'; but I do not find in them the official optimism and falsehoods which are customary in other more 'civilised' countries. On the contrary: in order to demand more effectively the great effort which is required, it seems to me that the danger is being deliberately overstated.

The meeting of the soviet is thinly attended. A number of its members are at the front. There are many army greatcoats, fur or leather jackets, revolvers on belts. Young women, workers, soldiers, Bashkirs.* Not a single intellectual in sight. It really is the people itself, the people which suffers, toils, labours, fights, the people with horny, chapped hands, the people which is inelegant, rough, a little brutal, with clumsy movements, with faces not refined by civilisation. Nobody speaks to reply or to ask questions. This is not the time for debating; in any case, the soviet does not debate much, there is nothing parliamentary about it. As it is at the moment, it is nothing but a very simple apparatus for popular consultation and dictatorship. By a show of hands, almost unanimously, they accept the sober and concise resolution which Zinoviev reads out. It can be summed up in four words: Struggle to the death.

Nonetheless, the assembly is not passive. Such acceptance on its own would be worrying. But now, as people are leaving, someone shouts out: *The Internationale*. The whole hall rises to its feet, bare-headed, and two thousand manly voices intone the song of the 'last fight'.

I have heard it sung by crowds many times before; but I don't think I have ever seen such faces, resolute despite the wrinkles of weariness and the pale, worn complexions produced by these days of privation. A man in front of me grips the back of a deputy's chair with his two broad, muscular hands; I observe his

---

* Muslims from the Southern Urals. *[Translator's note]*

rough face, the veins standing out on his neck, his broad-shouldered athletic build. Here are some Communist girls with short hair, young and old soldiers who have probably just come back from the front, and men of whom it is impossible to say whether or not they are soldiers, their uniform is so minimal.

They are all singing. Every person present here knows that perhaps this very evening they will be fighting in front of their own house, that they will perhaps be killed, that if they are taken alive they will be hanged, or shot, or tortured, that the city has only enough bread for twenty-four hours, that the greatest powers in the world, the Entente, America, are relentlessly seeking *their death* and that of all their comrades. That is why they are so simple, so solemn, standing upright, bare-headed, armed, raising their unanimous voices with such great fervour.

A humble crowd, they have the faith, the will, the indomitable inner energy of masses who have discovered spiritual life. Cromwell's Roundheads who founded the English republic, the Puritans and Quakers who built their homes on the sites that would later give birth to the opulent metropolises of the United States, the enthusiastic and stoical Calvinists who attempted, in the sixteenth century, throughout Europe, to achieve a moral and social revolution, must have been like this.

Slowly, following the rhythm of the singing, the crowd leaves the Tauride Palace. I think of the manly races which, in history, have taken on the role of beginning the human task afresh, on the bases of a new consciousness; the task of taking justice among men a step further forward. Chosen races, invincible and sacrificed. Oh! I understand that you are admired and also hated, Russian people, you who are unvanquished by poverty and fear, and who are going with all the energy of your immense strength, with your vast capacity for suffering, your patience, your endurance, your fervour, your elementary good sense, towards a goal which is so great—and still so distant—that the weak and cowardly will disown you, that the disillusioned will no longer believe in you, that the sceptics will mock you and that the great of this world will be afraid of you.

Moral force

And at certain moments one is profoundly aware that in the whole vast expanse of Russia, these men are the only ones in whom *moral force* resides. Disorganisation, chaos, material deprivation and weariness are factors which operate equally on both sides of the barricades. But the consciousness of the very lofty goal, the will to win, the determination to make use of everything in order to win, to refuse to retreat in face of any sacrifice, in a word *moral force*, the idealism of a new faith, this decisive factor operates only among us, for us. That is why the Reds are the stronger—permanently. In its eternal struggle against the Black and the Grey (the image is Gorky's) the Red, colour of blood, flame, ardour and life, must inevitably triumph. Officers who have been educated and disciplined, who dispose of financial resources, who possess the sophisticated techniques of modern warfare, can drive against us, under threat of death, terrified herds of soldiers—prisoners—or launch against us gangs of drunken Cossacks.

What they cannot achieve at any price is that young men and women, bearers of the little pass covered in brown cloth issued by the Communist PK *(Parteyni Komitet)*, should voluntarily put on the leather jacket and march into the gunfire singing *The Internationale*.

They have no ideal, they belong to a declining class, which has finished its task and must be replaced; we are those rising to replace them; that is why they cannot win, they can only kill.

Meanwhile Communists, workers, soldiers and *ad hoc* administrators are now working with feverish haste. In four days assistance has come from all parts of Russia. Zinoviev's radio-telegram which simply said 'Petrograd in danger!' has evoked responses from all over. Supply trains for destinations all over the country have come—without waiting for special instructions—to unload their stocks of food at the Nicholas Station. From Cherepovetz, from Novgorod, from Moscow, from Schlüsselburg, workers and Communists have hastened here, while the regular divisions of the Red army came by every route that was free. The most intense organisational work was carried out under enemy fire, under the determined leadership of Trotsky. Now that the surprise of the first moment has worn off, we understand that the enemy cannot win, that every hour lessens his chances.

Nonetheless, our forces have retreated to the hills of Pulkovo, the last line of defence. If they were to yield to another thrust, then we would be fighting in the suburbs. The surroundings of the Warsaw Station and the Narva Gate are being fortified in anticipation of a setback. Houses are transformed into fortresses, others are evacuated or demolished so as not to obstruct the line of fire from certain redoubts made of paving stones, firewood and sacks of earth built up at crossroads and dominating the streets. But a proclamation by Trotsky to the Red soldiers, to the commanders, to the commissars, urges them to go over to the offensive and announces to them—magic word—that *our* tanks will be going into action. The neutralisation of the enemy attacks, states Trotsky, is a portent of victory. It must be true: it is impossible to capture a city which resists like this.

On the streets

The whole of Petrograd gives an impression of intense labour. Redoubts and barricades are springing out of the earth. At the Field of Mars, around the tombs of the martyrs of the revolution, groups of men and women are at work, digging trenches in the light rain. In front of the Peter-Paul Fortress, at the entry from the Troitsky (Trinity) Bridge, the trenches are ready, carefully prepared, even to the extent that, when there are snipers, they will have somewhere to rest their elbows. A few metres in front, working women are stretching out barbed wire.

A great many such wooden barriers, intersecting with tangles of barbed wire, have been erected in the vegetable gardens of Smolny. Now they are everywhere, blocking all the main thoroughfares. In a quarter of an hour, they can be planted amid the paving stones. Here and there, through the streets, groups of workers, men and women, are carrying sacks of earth or logs. Especially at night, in certain places, forced labour is on the increase. Unfortunately it is forced labour: there are not enough Communists to do the work, and it has been necessary to requisition the labour force from among the citizens; the committees of assistance to the poor have each had to supply a few persons.

Nevsky Prospect looks almost the same as usual. There are more people moving around there. But if you approach the Admiralty gardens, you find, behind the railings, skilfully concealed by a curtain of bushes, the earth banked up round a redoubt and the mouth of a cannon aimed at the roadway. Further on, on the corner of the Sadovaia, they have taken advantage of the arcades of Gostinny Dvor, formerly a bazaar and the local commercial centre, to establish a guard-house surrounded on all sides with sacks of earth. The crossroads is confronted with ambushes on three sides.

Right at the other end of Nevsky Prospect, at Znamensky Square, you notice nothing to begin with. The massive bronze effigy of Alexander II looms up opposite the station. Enormous, heavy, the horseman with broad loins and a weighty jaw, mournful, his head lowered, is pushing forward his stocky horse which is visibly incapable of going any further. The sculptor, prince Trubestskoi, was a powerful ironist who erected in the very middle of imperial Petersburg this symbol of the impotent autocracy, bleakly halted at the edge of the abyss, massive but without strength! Today, the symbol has acquired a significant commentary. There is, to the left behind the bronze statue, a hollow dug out in the ground of the square, surrounded by a small, low barricade in wood and stone. Here there is a cannon to provide enfilading fire over the Ligovskaia, where the enemy would appear if they got that far.

Lev Davidovich Trotsky

Along Nevsky Prospect came two cars which stopped because of an obstacle. Amid the crowd of passers-by, brief signals were exchanged. A name was spread from mouth to mouth. Two open cars. It was the second one that I noticed first, large and clean with its black seats upholstered and comfortable. Seven or eight men in black leather jackets were standing in it, with guns in their hands. Their headgear struck me; they were wearing a sort of helmet made of felt or covered with stout green uniform cloth, with a high rounded point and decorated with the great red five-pointed star. It recalled the headgear of the Slav warriors in heroic times (but what times were more heroic than ours?).

Trotsky, I was told. And I glimpsed him in the first car, wearing the same headgear low over his eyes, and the grey coat worn by all soldiers. By his frown, by the eyeglasses behind which his sharp, dark gaze is concealed, by his little moustache and the beard on his chin, he can always be recognised immediately.

At this moment he was frowning; his expression was stern, a little bothered. I knew of his strenuous activity, his nights spent at Smolny with the executive committee of the soviet in permanent session, his trips to the front, and genuine anecdotes which later will become myth. Somewhere in the south, during a cavalry raid by General Mamontov (who recently laid waste Tambov, Koslov and Eletz) his train was surrounded by a band of Cossacks; he had to fight them and came off victoriously. During those days, at the front, Lev Davidovich slept in the trenches in the front line. It once happened that he arrived in a car when the Reds were being routed. The enemy was advancing and our men were fleeing in panic. Lev Davidovich leapt onto a horse and drove those fleeing back to face the enemy—or else himself led them into the attack, I'm not sure of the details. This personal courage is sometimes actually criticised as being rather imprudent in an organiser and a leader.

In these stories which are spread by word of mouth, how much is the product of popular imagination? I don't care. If these precise details are not true, then other similar ones, which are unknown, certainly are true. The man before us is the organiser of a revolutionary army. He has made this army out of nothing: out of the nothingness of confused crowds of soldiers in revolt against the war, who seized trains by force, and, becoming peasants once again, were irresistibly going back to the land.

What a surprising and strong multifaceted personality which no one would have expected in this journalist, theoretician and agitator, whose typical intellectual's face today seems so forceful.

He has a high forehead, and the way he holds his head is a little stiff, perhaps forced—in order to command you have to stand up very straight, with the head raised aloft, all the weariness of the past energetically shrugged off; there is a thin, powerful mouth like a bird of prey above the chin which seems very short when at rest; the three commas, moustache and goatee, give his face a Mephistophelean expression. I remember the broad, precise, affirmative, imperative gestures of the orator, his voice which declaims sentences as one would hammer a malleable metal, giving a clear sound; his threatening irony which gives the impression of a rapier blow aimed into the dark and hitting its target.

I don't want to exaggerate. Leaders are forced on me, I don't want idolatry towards them. I see in them the first servants of the proletariat, those who must be followed, but those too who must always be looked in the face with the eyes of a free man. But it seems to me that Petrograd really feels it is saved now that this leader has come.

The law of the sword

Here, today, Lev Davidovich Trotsky is the soul of the resistance. If, a few miles from here, the attack waves are being reformed and methodically launched into action, if trainloads of meat and ammunition, if all the forces of this poor exhausted country are being strained, organised and used systematically in the interests of victory, it is because they are channelled by his intelligence and directed by his will. It is a hard job! Siberian front, Ukrainian front, Polish and Latvian front, Petrograd front, Karelian front, Archangel front. The front of a civil war in the interior. A cruel job for the man who must think of everything and who must, as a revolutionary, act ruthlessly. This evening I read an order by Trotsky, laying down that the families of officers and Red soldiers who have gone over to the enemy must be immediately arrested and treated as hostages. The names follow. Today they have arrested Marfa Andreevna and her daughter Vera, wife and daughter of X, a traitor who has gone over to the enemy.

Kill or be killed: the Commune also, the Commune which writes on its banners such elevated ideas, knows this old law of the sword.

At the Peter-Paul Fortress

We cross the Troitsky bridge. On both sides the Neva widens out, its rolling waves the colour of sea-water. Opposite opens up Kameno-Ostrovsky Prospect, lined with the homes and gardens of the wealthy, now expropriated. Somewhere here, in the little palace belonging to a ballerina who was the Tsar's mistress, Vladimir Ilyich worked, waiting to give the signal for the end of the old society. Here are the low, blue pinnacle turrets of Chinese appearance belonging to a little church dating from the days of Peter the Great: when this church was built the city scarcely existed. Further on, like an enormous sapphire placed on the tree tops, the cupola of the mosque, the minarets like exclamation marks. Our beautiful city!

We cross the drawbridge, and pass through an ugly portico built in red brick which is well guarded. A path opens up with a double row of old trees and antiquated single-storey guardhouses, yellow façades which could be taken for peaceful country dwellings. It is an idyllic scene. We are in the precincts of the Peter-Paul Fortress. Along this path, all the proud spirits and hearts beating with youth that Russia has known for the last century have passed, on their way to prison, penal servitude, torture and death. Names flood into the memory in confused fashion: The Decembrists, Nechayev, Chernyshevsky, Bakunin, Lavrov, the *narodnovoltsy*, Kaliaev, Lenin's brother who was hanged. The gilded spire of the church impassively looms over all these memories. How many eyes, lost to life, were drawn to that spire during their short exercise periods in the prison?

Everything must be paid for! Grand-dukes, generals, admirals, bankers, plutocrats, ministers, dignitaries, a whole opulent crowd, laden with honours, passed by here, beaten, spattered with mud, shameful, wretched, before suffering the implacable law that they had taught us.

Now, in one of these unassuming old buildings, where the rooms are tiny and the corridors so narrow that you can't walk two abreast, in the largest room I saw our local commander, Avrov, working. Around his office there is a network of telephone apparatuses, where the wearisome ringing scarcely ever stops. Avrov is a young man. Perhaps thirty-five? A very open face, broad at the top and tapering down to an angular chin. A face with delicate features, like a refined peasant. His eyes seemed grey to me. I don't know whether they noticed me while we were talking. Little drops of sweat were forming on his temples, on his swollen veins. The collar of his tunic was unbuttoned as if this man for whom command had become a harsh physical task, were struggling against a feeling of being suffocated. It is the city, I thought, which he feels is suffocating with every throb of his veins.

As I leave his office, a comrade shows me a map of Petrograd marked in various places with signs in blue pencil. This map was captured one night not long ago less than fifteen minutes from this headquarters. The marked points indicate where the enemy within intended to strike us.

Reversal

These things are possible only in Russia. These things are possible only during a revolution. During hurricanes, there are sudden moments of calm. Here there is calm amid the storm. Especially in tropical regions where intense, burning, feverish life hastens constantly to die and be reborn, these sudden changes are, it is said, miraculous. The glorious sunshine pours out over the plains and forests which, only a moment ago, were battered by ferocious winds, whipped by rainstorms and shaken by the raging of the elements. The unforeseen regains its capricious rights in societies which are prey to the unleashing of opposing forces.

Normal time no longer exists
For the mad and resolute hearts
Of these hyperbolic crowds.

These fine lines by Verhaeren come into my memory as I think of the amazing contrast between this Russian life today and any normal life at the present time in the so-called civilised world—or even here, scarcely two years ago.

This morning, 30 October, a total change in the situation— which was beginning to become apparent over the last two days— becomes clear and asserts itself. Petrograd is indeed saved! The Red republic is saved! On three vast fronts, a series of victories, so unexpected and inexplicable to the outside eye that they seem miraculous, have turned the situation round.

Krasnoe Selo, Pavlovsk, Tsarkoe, Gatchina on the outskirts of Petrograd have been recaptured. Now the White gangs will have to retreat hastily to Yamburg or Narva. And in addition their communications are threatened by the Red cavalry which, having recaptured Luga, is closing on Gdov, hitherto the inaccessible lair of the 'National army'.

Similar news from the southern front. We have the initiative in the fighting. Orel and Voronezh have been recaptured, Denikin's offensive has quite *unquestionably* been broken. The Red troops are advancing on Kursk.

And far over there, on the Siberian front, beyond the summits of the Urals, the Communist army, which has just recaptured Tobolsk, is undertaking an offensive against Omsk.

We are a starving country, exhausted by more than five terrible years; for nearly two years we have endured a blockade which has not allowed a spool of thread or a tin of food to enter our territory; we are the most sorely tried, the worst fed, the most ill-clothed, the worst heated people on earth. Horses fall over and die of hunger in our streets (and sometimes people too). Why do they need British and French tanks, or international military missions?

The European strategists and armchair politicians who, for two years, have been predicting that Lenin and Trotsky would be hanged 'within a week' will understand nothing of it. For it is psychologically impossible for them to understand anything about the revolution. Nourished on 'normal' bourgeois culture and incapable of understanding the profound historical causes of the class struggle which they approach blindly, even more incapable of conceiving, with their miserable brains and their desiccated hearts, the reality of a class's determination, they drag up childish explanations for this new phase of the great revolutionary drama.

What 'German officers' are they going to invent to put them at the head of our Red troops? What Chinese or Latvian fusiliers will they claim were defending Petrograd?

In fact an issue of *Pravda*, of which the whole second page is devoted to obituaries, will one day give history the very simple solution to the enigma. *Pravda* names a few of those who have just fallen on the Petrograd front, the flower of the militants amid the heroic crowds. There is Justin Zhuk, a worker from the Schlüsselberg factories, an anarcho-syndicalist, unit commissar, killed on the Finnish frontier; Vladimir Mazin, intellectual, formerly a Menshevik, on the editorial staff of *Communist International*, commissar of the Sixth Division, killed at Kipen; the

Communist worker Chekalov and many, many others.

Did all those men go to war *because* they had been called up? But it was they who organised the call-up: for ten years, in some cases for twenty, these men gave their freedom, their life to the revolutionary task. They foresaw and accepted this outcome. And when such men are leading a people which is defending its vital interests, the freshly won gains of a social revolution, when they do everything themselves, everything: the work of the factories, the railways, the military command, the schools, and war—then they certainly can be killed, but they can never be defeated.

The party's effort

Various scenes glimpsed in the street during these difficult days explain many things. While equivocal Communists were disappearing, the sector committees in the city were gaining several thousand new recruits amidst the danger. At least it cannot be said that these were motivated by self-interest. They constitute indisputable evidence of devotion and trust towards the soviet regime, defended by the Bolshevik party. I understood what these new recruits meant in practice when I saw, outside the premises of a committee, about a hundred women workers from factories and offices, still poorly clad like working women, queuing up for a roll-call before leaving for the front. For the front, where they were to give a very good account of themselves. So we may have been short of medical supplies, of bandages, of stretchers—for those could be taken away from us—but the dedication of the women was not absent. And that was the main thing.

The whole party has made an immense effort, supported by the entire working population, that is by all the energetic elements in the population. This effort, and the social and moral causes responsible for it, explain everything. The party at this time is the only organisation capable of inspiring, channelling and directing the energies which have just triumphed (and moreover let us note that it maintains its unique situation in dictatorial fashion), but it is nonetheless true that they exist outside it, that they constitute its strength only because it represents them knowingly, because it is, in short, *only one of the means* of the revolution, in some sense the most powerful lever of the proletariat. A truth which is all the more obvious in that the revolution also makes use of enemies of the party.

The party? I have long sought to define its role in relation to the class and the revolution. Here, at such times, this role seems to be self-evident. The party is in a sense the nervous system of the class. Simultaneously the consciousness and the active, physical organisation of all the dispersed forces of the proletariat, which are often ignorant of themselves and often remain latent or express themselves contradictorily.

The anarchists

This is the appropriate point to note that the anarchists, the Anarchist Federation of Petrograd, short of militants because it has sent the best of its forces to the front and to the Bolshevik party, has found itself, in these solemn days, as in the time of Kerensky, entirely on the side of the party. Not without critical attitudes and not without friction. The anarchist manifesto flyposted in the streets began with a reference—both very much deserved and terribly unjust—to the 'soldiers, mobilised by force, who are now fleeing before the enemy', and called on revolutionaries to contribute freely, as partisans, to the defence of Petrograd. Anarchist partisans, formed into two or three select groups, strong in their close mutual understanding, were among the first to be at their posts. During the first night of danger (24-25 October), the anarchists, almost the only ones to be completely ready, came, by a curious irony of circumstances, to occupy, in order to defend them if necessary, the premises of *Pravda*, the intransigent Marxism of which is rather hostile towards them. What did that mean, except that in face of the common enemy, the great revolutionary family—where there are so many enemy brothers—is one; and that at the most critical moments, class instinct wins out over ideological deviations and sectarian spirit?

In these times of struggle, the most serious divergences of opinion become secondary; for the very life of the first socialist society is at stake.

A gesture

However, the anarchist spirit—with its perpetual flights towards Utopia and their usual disastrous consequences in practice—has not lost its influence over its supporters, even when good sense comes out on top. In this connection here is a very significant episode.

The headquarters of the body of anarchist volunteers was situated five minutes away from the Nicholas Station, in a wrecked flat on the ground floor of a tall, grey building. In general anyone who wanted to could enter this anarchist club where nobody was checked other than on the basis of personal contacts. When they organised to fight, anyone who wanted to could turn up. A few strangers appeared. 'We're anarchists too,' they said, 'against all forms of power, against all authority, for the total revolution.' The great family of this hundred or so idealists welcomed them without question. They were given their allocation of cartridges and grenades. Then one day, by chance, comrades found some bombs in the club, very probably intended to blow them all up. Suspicion fell on two of the newcomers. Here began the absurd dilemma of anarchism and reality. The suspects were arrested and locked up. An armed sentry was put at the door of the room where they were imprisoned. They were interrogated and tried. The anarchists who did that were horrified and heartbroken at having to do it. 'Here we are like members of the Cheka!' they said with remorseful smiles. They saw the brutal necessity of scorning their own generous metaphysical principles. *('Thou shalt not judge!')* But the case was a serious one. Two Whites confessed—more or less.

Should they be executed? In Makhno's organisation nobody would have hesitated for five seconds. The Petrograd anarchists, to extricate themselves from the quandary, adopted the most unsatisfactory solution; they decided to hand the two suspects over to the local military commander. In their own minds nobody doubted that the latter would have them shot immediately.

My good comrade B.† was given the job of taking them to the Peter-Paul Fortress. Thin, tubercular, consumed by activity,

---

* In *Memoirs of a Revolutionary* B. is identified as Kolabushkin.
[Translator's note]

agile, alert, eloquent, confused, with handsome blue eyes, child-like and bubbling with enthusiasm, B. during his long life as a revolutionary had done ten years penal servitude. His courage stood up to all tests and his loyalty was such that the Petrograd soviet had complete confidence in him. He told me himself what strange emotion he was gripped by when he found himself, a revolver in his belt, sitting opposite two pale-faced prisoners in the car making its way to the Peter-Paul Fortress, which meant prison and death for these men.

From time to time he cast a glance out of the car windows onto the road as it sped by. And he recalled the day when he himself had been arrested and taken in the same way to the same fortress, through the very same streets. They were coming up to the Troitsky Bridge. The gilt spire of Peter-Paul was already silhouetted against the sky above the pillboxes. 'And now I'm the one, I'm the person taking men who are going to be executed!' thought B., his nerves on edge. He thought he was going to choke. They were nearly there.

'Stop!' he shouted to the driver.

The car stopped two hundred metres from the gateway of the fortress. B. must have been more overwhelmed than his prisoners. He quickly opened the door and waved his arm towards the deserted street:

'Off you go!'

'You can't imagine,' he said to me afterwards, 'what relief I felt at that moment.'

Yes I can. In an way I do understand this action. Haven't I too suffered years of imprisonment? But this act seems to me to be mad, a peculiar libertarian madness. Was it not a crime to release White terrorists onto the streets of Red Petrograd?

If it had occurred at all frequently, such magnanimity would have meant the suicide of the revolution. The success of a revolution requires the implacable severity of a Dzerzhinsky—who of course was an ex-convict himself.

SIX WEEKS have gone by since those epic, nightmare days. The victory of the Reds has been magnificently confirmed. The second anniversary of the October revolution could be celebrated, soberly, in an atmosphere of strength and confidence.

Since then, in about forty days, Western Siberia up to Tomsk and the Ukraine—Kiev, Kharkov, Poltava—right up the Don, have been recaptured.

What remains of the 'national army' of the north-western government is struggling before the walls of Narva in an iron grip. In certain White Russian newspapers published in Finland the defeat of Yudenich is being openly discussed. Incapacity in command, red tape, arbitrariness, abuse of authority by the NCOs, lack of foresight. These are the explanations given. When they got to Gatchina, the Whites, far from being able to feed the population whom they had come to 'liberate', did not have any bread left themselves. Thus, in the tiny pond where the toads of the old order, who also 'want a king', croak, all the mistakes of Tsarism, of Lyao-Yang, of Tsushima,* of Poland, of Galicia, of Rumania, are being committed again. These émigrés, like those of yesteryear, have learned nothing and forgotten nothing.

But they have taught us how to put up barricades; on the approaches to Smolny, there is a proper redoubt made of sacks of earth, equipped inside with an armoured telephone post; it is still waiting for the return of the two cannon which have just been removed. Now it is covered with snow. And we have a picturesque image with an epic touch to it of all these fortifications—calling to mind the thought of a far-sighted and wise uprising—scattered in the city which is infinitely peaceful under its cloak of snow.

Petrograd, November-December 1919

Yudenich: What happened on the other side of the front?

On the subject of the 'battle of Petrograd' we possess two books written by our enemies. One of them, which is unreadable, is by Major-General A-P Rodzianko; the other, *At the Gates of Petrograd*, is overdetailed and confused; it is by Mr Kirdetsov who experienced the campaign as editor of a semi-official White newspaper. He provides us with ample and instructive documentation.

---

* Russian defeats in the Russo-Japanese war (1904-05).
[Translator's note]

In the circle of iron and fire

Here is the military situation in the Soviet Republic in the summer of 1919. Generals Miller and Ironside, supported by British and American troops, are occupying Archangel and Murmansk, and moving down towards Chenkursk. The Latvians, backed up by von der Goltz's ruffians, have just taken Riga. The Poles are occupying Mozyr. Kolchak is advancing on Samara and Kazan. Denikin is occupying the Kuban and the Don country, and is advancing. Petlura, Makhno and Grigoriev are devastating the Ukraine. Between Narva and Pskov, to the south west of Petrograd, the White army of the northwest, led by the cut-throats Rodzianko (Major General) and Bulak-Balakhovich, is in control of the countryside. On 1 January the British fleet appeared in the Gulf of Finland, sinking one Red destroyer and capturing two, the *Spartacus* and the *Astroil*, which Admiral Cowan handed over to the Estonian government. The circle of iron and fire is complete and has been closed. Lord Churchill and M. Pichon* are full of hope. 'The Bolsheviks, we'll have them!' '*All the reformist Socialists,*' writes Mr Kirdetsov, '*are in favour of intervention.*'

In May and June, Rodzianko attempted an attack on Petrograd. His forces were made up of reactionary officers, the Russian mercenaries of Count Livien, equipped and trained by von der Goltz, and Bulak-Balakhovich's cavalry. The national army of the northwest took Pskov, Yamburg and Gdov, leaving bodies dangling from gallows along its route. It was a war of banditry and treachery: Semenov's Red regiment, undermined by the Social Revolutionaries, cut the throats of its commissars and went over to the Whites; the Krasnaia Gorka fort was handed over to them at one point by officers who had pretended to rally to the cause of the soviets.[4]

On 14 June, an edict from Admiral Kolchak, the Supreme Ruler, appointed Yudenich as Commander-in-Chief of the northwest. Yudenich? He is the hero—by accident—of Erzurum. 'A gentleman aged about fifty, stocky, with a bloated face, bull neck and drooping moustache'; he is a worthless person, of limited

---

* Stephen Pichon (1857-1933); French Foreign Minister 1917-20; a signatory of the Versailles Treaty. *[Translator's note]*

capacity, incapable of initiative or of any flash of intelligence. But he knows how to obey when it is a question of restoring order. A perfect hangman if required. He lives at Helsinki, surrounded by former leading figures of the Russian reactionary milieu such as Kartachev and Kuzmin-Karavaev, in the 'unbearable atmosphere of espionage created by the Entente agents'. Behind him are two high authorities: Kolchak who left Siberia dripping with blood, and the Paris National Conference, a sort of émigré government in exile, in which could be found side by side former lackeys of Tsarism, Sazonov and Isvolsky (the men of 1 August 1914), the former Social Revolutionary terrorist Savinkov, Kerensky's former ambassadors Bekhmetiev and Maklakov, the former 'revolutionary' scholar Chaikovsky; in short, a coalition of all the reactionary forces. A French destroyer brought Yudenich to his troops, from Helsinki to Estonia.

Finland and Estonia

The Finnish frontier is 25 miles from Petrograd, the Estonian frontier 75. In Finland the murderous Mannerheim holds power, after having barbarically crushed the Communist rising in 1918. His White Guards number 120,000 battle-hardened and extremely well-armed men. The Germans, formerly called on for assistance by the President of the Republic, Svinhufvud, left behind them when they departed stocks of arms and ammunition. French officers from the Etiévant mission are organising their general staff. But above all Finland is concerned to ensure its national independence. It does not forget that Kerensky appointed a governor-general over it, and notes that the Bolsheviks, on the other hand, recognised its right of self-determination. A decisively clever move, as we shall see. Class interest, hatred of the 'Reds', drives White Finland to co-operate with the capture of Petrograd. But after that? What power will be established in the Russian capital? Monarchists and gentlemen like Kartachev and Kuzmin-Karavaev, Yudenich's advisers, refuse, like Admiral Kolchak, to recognise Finland's independence, although it is recognised by France, Italy, Britain and the United States. The 'democratic' Paris conference makes the same refusal. 'The future pan-Russian Constituent Assembly will alone be

empowered to grant independence to states bordering on Russia';
such is the polite, diplomatic formulation of an unyielding refusal.
Shameless looters, the Finnish bourgeoisie have confiscated,
contrary to all legal rights, Russian ships in their ports, Russian
property (even that of the Red Cross) on their territory. That is
what they mean by respect for private property. Any bourgeois
government established in Petrograd would call them to account.
Isn't it better for them to let Russia be consumed by internal
struggles and then take advantage of its weakness? This policy is
considered to be the wise one, and is challenged only by those
industrialists and merchants who used to live on trade with Russia,
to which they sold paper and from which they bought grain which
America is now selling them at high prices. So Finland is
perplexed. It also has good reason to fear its own working class,
defeated but still formidable. It hesitates to engage in all-out war
against the Bolsheviks, but in Karelia it gives free rein to its
adventurers, its imperialist students, and the gangs of Elven Greye
which are regularly beaten by the Communists.

The situation is the same in Estonia. Here the republic owes
its existence to Britain—and it almost had to pay dear for it.
'Without vigorous interventions by Clemenceau, the British
would have grabbed the islands of Oesel [Saare Maa] and Dagoe
[Hiiu Maa]', writes Kirdetsov. The Social Democrats are
influential in the coalition cabinet. One of them, Mr Rey, is chair
of the constituent assembly. Estonia, speaking in the voice of
statesmen it has just discovered—Tennison, Piip, Poska—is
worried by the reluctance of the Paris Conference and of
Yudenich's advisers. It is asking for guarantees of peace and
autonomy after the fall of the Bolsheviks. Nobody among the
White émigrés would dream of granting them. The Populist
Socialist Chaikovsky one day said brutally to the Estonian
plenipotentiaries: 'Russia needs Tallinn.'

The bourgeois reactionary bloc, cobbled together against
Bolshevism, is therefore undermined by irresoluble internal
contradictions. The Estonian and Finnish petty-bourgeoisies
cannot renounce national independence, and the large and small
bourgeoisie in Russia cannot renounce their imperialist ambitions.
The conflict between British and French influence in the Baltic,

and the clumsy inflexibility of the Russian reactionary leaders completely compromise the cohesion of the Whites.

The British General Marsh *

These contradictions are too deep to be resolved by negotiations. The Reds, on the other hand, are hard at work, and the situation at the front is becoming desperate.

Then the British General Marsh intervenes.

Until this moment Yudenich has exercised unchallenged power. At the request of the political conference at Helsinki, France is putting pressure on Finland, to which she is sending tanks and aeroplanes. From New York, Mr Hoover is supplying the Russian army of the northwest on behalf of the future provisional government *while reserving to himself the control of the distribution of supplies.* But everything is in danger. So they have to act quickly—capture Petrograd—for the Estonians are not concealing the fact that they will make peace with the Bolsheviks (who are offering it to them) rather than fight another winter campaign.

General Marsh has decided to resolve all difficulties, just as he would do in the Sudan or in Persia, but according to good old democratic traditions. On 10 August he convenes at his headquarters—one hour in advance!—some leading Russian figures from Tallinn and gives them forty minutes to form a democratic government. These gentlemen accept. The north western government is formed. Mr Lianozov, a large industrialist and oilman, is the president; around him are intellectuals and socialists (two Mensheviks, two Social Revolutionaries). Yudenich becomes Minister of War.

To this government, the British military man dictates his programme: democratic government (of course!), a solution to the land question by the Constituent Assembly, social legislation and the eight-hour day (!), democratic freedoms, recognition of Estonian independence. Moreover, the ministers write to the soldiers in the army:

'We are not a government of capitalists and landlords. We

---

* Brigadier General Frank Graham Marsh (1875-1957). *[Translator's note]*

represent all classes in society. We shall not tolerate a return to the old order'; which proves that Communist propaganda is having an effect, even on this side of the front. Kolchak and the Paris conference will not be happy. But General Marsh and the Estonians are satisfied, and for the time being that is the most important thing.

Meanwhile at Pskov, the British Captain Peary-Gordon is organising a democratic conference. The Russians must be emancipated!

A democratic government

Nothing is more distressing than the sight of the northwestern government. It has no territory, or virtually none: the scrap of Russia occupied by the White army is a military zone governed by Commander-in-Chief Yudenich. He doesn't have a halfpenny; he cannot do anything at all. His ministers have to hand out their appeals to the soldiers themselves, and they are happy to be tolerated despite their liberal language.

The story of his finances is altogether woeful. Kolchak granted to Yudenich—before the formation of the government which he did not want to know about—a sum of 900,000 pounds sterling, deposited in a bank in London. Yudenich hastened to issue banknotes worth 500 million roubles. The government let it be understood that these notes were guaranteed, not by funds deposited in Britain, but by the British government itself, and got a sharp repudiation from the Foreign Office. Then it lived on its notes, while Yudenich spent the money—so imprudently that when the collapse came, he had only 250,000 pounds left in the till (and the arms, ammunition and supplies were provided by the Allies on credit, to be paid for by the future Russian regime). The Yudenich notes were sold, at the end of the adventure, for the price of waste paper, to an Estonian papermaker.

And what was happening in the territory of the northwestern government? We can hear it described by Mr Kirdetsov, who was in the confidence of the ministers in Tallinn. In a country liberated from the Bolsheviks, they applied the laws in force in wartime *in occupied enemy countries*. 'It's an orgy and it is virtually total ruin. Everywhere, it is the arbitrary rule of bandit

leaders.' The army was selling American flour at high prices to the
starving population—flour which did not belong to it, since it had
been bought by a council of state. At Pskov, Bulak-Balakhovich
was forging Kerensky government banknotes. At Yamburg, Pskov
and Gdov, they were executing in the streets people who were
suspect of sympathising with the Reds; these were dying in their
hundreds, tortured and then hanged. In the countryside, they
were requisitioning grain, potatoes, cattle.

A national army

How about the army? It was destitute, wretched, looted by
quartermasters who were all of them thieves and imbeciles.
Clothing, supplied in abundance by the Allies, was going to the
dodgers behind the lines; at the front, half the men were in rags.
For 18,000 fighting men, they had 109,000 pairs of boots, six
times more than were needed. But half the soldiers didn't have
any. At the rear, the food stores were full of tins, but the soldiers
went hungry. A crook, or the willing tool of crooks, General
Ianov, head of the supplies department, demanded food for
200,000 men, when he had a total of 70,000 mouths to feed. For
as against 18,000 ill-fed fighting men, there were more than
50,000 'conscripts' or idlers eating well at the rear. Transport was
bad. This was due to negligence: they had bought motor lorries,
but no petrol! Then they bought petrol at Copenhagen, too late
and at ruinous prices. Likewise they bought aeroplanes that were
paid for, but never delivered. All these abuses were subsequently
discovered by a commission inspecting the accounts, which, when
the army's debts had been paid, had only five million Estonian
marks left in its possession.

This small army of the robbed and this large army of
robbers had fifty-three generals on active service, among them the
former *ataman* Krasnov, Glazenap and the typical figure of
Vladimirov (his real name was Novogrebelsky). The latter, a very
influential figure, was the head of the political police and of
counter-espionage. He sometimes published forged manifestos in
the name of the revolutionary council of the Red army. He drew
up in advance a list of undesirable elements who would not be
allowed to enter Petrograd, and he advised Yudenich to include

the entire government on it. He formed teams of reliable men, with motor cars, who would be responsible, as soon as the Whites entered Petrograd, for the *small but necessary bloodletting*.

Victory and collapse

The offensive began on 28 September with an attack using tanks, and was crowned with victory (the British had sent six tanks). On 6 October, after an uninterrupted victorious march, the Whites arrived at the gates of Petrograd, at Gatchina. Then they took Tsarkoe Selo. Yudenich, confident of victory, ordered supplies to be sent urgently to Petrograd.

Already a horde of speculators and predators were settling on the outskirts of Petrograd. The representative of a British consortium of banks had arrived to set up an Anglo-Russian issuing bank in the capital. Buildings on the Nevsky Prospect were being bought and sold. Business was booming. The Estonian mark was falling and the Yudenich currency was rising.

At this very time Denikin was arriving at Orel, threatening the arsenals of Tula, the last bulwark of Moscow. Anxious to get its share in the impending rush for spoils, Finland was about to join in. The Social Democrat Horn, member of the northwestern government, was there whipping up public opinion. Finland asked only for the reimbursement, guaranteed by the Allies, of its campaign expenses, namely fifty million francs: business is business.

Then suddenly, from one day to the next, on 20 October, after the successes of the previous day, there was a collapse.

'The Bolsheviks revealed the diabolical cunning whereby they get themselves out of the most difficult situations by intensive propaganda and vigorous military actions; while our army was never ready. Contrary to Yudenich's predictions, there were never any disturbances or strikes in Petrograd, because neither the workers nor the supporters of liberal democracy in the city were really convinced that the northwestern government would bring them *Freedom, Bread and People's Power*. On the other hand, Trotsky immediately succeeded in bringing together reserves from all over the place, and formed enthusiastic battalions of worker Communists. According to the evidence of Yudenich's general staff, these battalions, the sailors and the trainee officers, fought like lions.' Kirdetsov, from whom I have quoted these lines, also speaks of 'Trotsky's consuming energy'. On 20 October, the Reds went on to the offensive at Pulkovo, a few miles from Petrograd.

'After our first successes,' Kirdetsov goes on to say, 'we had the feeling that victory would now be easy. There was general rejoicing. At the first setbacks, on the other hand, the command was completely demoralised'. Co-ordination was deplorably inadequate. Yudenich did not know where his different units were to be found. Defeat caught him unawares.

The Reds began a double movement turning to the north through Krasnaia Korba and to the south through Dno. On 8 November Gdov was taken. On 14 November Yamburg fell. Yudenich left the front, handing command over to Glazenap. The Estonians, who definitely wanted peace with the soviets, disarmed what remained of the White army, which was broken down, starving and demoralised: 14,000 victims of typhus filled the isolation hospitals and the cemeteries. The healthy ones were dumped in concentration camps, without shelter, in twenty degrees of frost, or sent to work in the forest, with conditions like slave plantations.

The causes

Why this collapse? Our authors complain of the inactivity of the British fleet and the unexpected activity of the Red fleet; of Yudenich's improvidence; of the attack by the Russo-German monarchist mercenary Bermont-Avalov on Riga, an attack which obliged the Estonians to turn against the new enemy; of the rivalries between White generals. They refer to the case of General Vietrenko who, when given the job of cutting the railway line between Petrograd and Moscow at Tosno, preferred to march on Petrograd in order that nobody else should get there before him; he thus left the road clear for the reinforcements called for by Trotsky.

Doubtless all these factors have some importance. But we know enough to recognise other immediate causes which were much more important, as well as other deep underlying causes which led to the collapse of the Whites.

It was mad to believe in the victory of a small army representing a caste (a military caste) led by the men of the old order who were not even trusted by the bourgeoisie, led by an aged imbecile with long military experience, invested with unlimited authority; an army which brought back the gallows of the old order and which reinstated its detested police force, its senile bureaucracy and its customs made intolerable by the distortions and exaggerations of wartime; an army which was facing a great working-class city where thousands and thousands of poor people were conscious of fighting simultaneously for their lives and for their ideals.

Yudenich's army had behind it nothing but Estonia, tiny and hostile. Petrograd had behind it the vast expanse of Red Russia. There were adventurers, mercenaries, a caste, a grey herd of soldiers driven to the slaughter. On the other side was a conscious revolutionary class. On one side was the old Yudenich, the hangman Rodzianko, mediocrities like Glazenap and Vladimirov; on the other the likes of Trotsky and Avrov who embodied youth and energy, the Communists.

Finally, through its internal divisions, through the inner rivalries inherent in capitalist society, through all the faults of the old regime with which it was weighed down, the Russian counter-revolution, at the gates of Petrograd as elsewhere, was inevitably condemned in advance. Moreover, it was facing the greatest material and moral force of the century: the interests and the consciousness of a class to which the future belongs. The British fleet did not intervene because British working class opinion would not have tolerated its intervention.

ALL THIS is rich in lessons. We draw attention to the total powerlessness of bourgeois democracy within the counter-revolution, as well as the participation and role of 'Socialists' in the northwestern government.

Notes

1   The movement collapsed on 19 July; the Barcelona general strike was postponed and was finally defeated in August.

2   A Russian word which is difficult to translate. It refers to the fearful petty-bourgeoisie.

3   Tsarkoe Selo, literally village of the Tsar, has been turned into Dietskoe Selo, village of children.

4   I have given an account of these events in one of the *Cahiers du travail* which appeared in 1921, *During the Civil War*.

The anarchists and the experience
of the Russian revolution

Preface: The following study, which is excessively brief and schematic, was written in great haste in 1920, after long and vigorous arguments with militants who had come to Russia for the Second Congress of the Communist International, in particular with comrades Lepetit, Vergeat, Pestaña and Armando Borghi. I'm sure that all these comrades were more or less in agreement with me on the whole set of ideas presented below. Since then, other less well-known French and Spanish libertarians who have visited Red Russia have had the opportunity of expressing their approval. So much so that it now seems to me to be a general principle: foreign anarchists who come to Russia, especially those who are active in the labour movement in their native country, immediately endorse the principle of the revolutionary dictatorship and accept its implications.

As far as the Russian anarchists are concerned, several well-known militants have to my knowledge clearly endorsed this principle: in particular the anarcho-syndicalist comrade Grossman-Roshchin, of *Golos Truda* (The Voice of Labour); Gordin, an anarchist-universalist; and Perkus, a Russian anarchist who was repatriated from America. Obviously there is no need to mention here those who actually joined the Russian Communist party.

Since these pages were written, the awesome experience of the first social revolution of modern times has continued to develop with relentless logic. Today we are the witnesses of the tragedy of a social revolution being contained within national frontiers, as a result of the passivity of the peoples of Europe faced with intelligent and well-armed reactionary forces. It is thus stifled and reduced to playing for time with the enemy within and without. We have seen many mistakes made, many errors revealed, and from the libertarian point of view many precious truths have been confirmed. It seems to me that libertarian thought emerges further strengthened from this experience of an additional year—on condition that having revised traditional ideas, we are willing to look at things from the standpoint of historical realism,[1] to take account of the needs of the masses and of the major factors of international economic and psychological life, the course of which depends much more on actual events than on our dreams and aspirations.

In short, the reform of anarchism that I should like to advocate is as follows: instead of being a subjective doctrine which is too inexorable and indeed largely Utopian, it should be brought back to the reality of the class struggle and its practical necessities, though without losing anything of its ethical value for the individual or for the social movement (quite the reverse should be the case). It must cease being the privileged possession of tiny sectarian groupings and contribute to the fullness and richness of the vast working-class movement destined to carry through social transformation by passing through the necessary stage of communism.

After a year of fresh experiences, many things should be added to this work which is too short and condensed. But since I am not able to revise it, I address it as it stands to the comrades. In its general outline it seems to me to be more true and more accurate today than it was a year ago; for it is all the more topical in that, in several countries, a number of anarchist militants believe they are obliged to adopt a sharply hostile attitude towards the proletarian dictatorship in Russia, generally revealing thereby a lack of experience and an attachment to tradition which are fraught with danger. The elementary truths set out here are therefore well worth repeating: we have to give birth to the new anarchism which, in the forthcoming revolutionary struggles, instead of complicating situations and making the internal upheavals of the revolution even worse, will contribute to elevating, ennobling and enlightening the spirit of the communism of the future.

The libertarian movement abroad must avoid repeating the catastrophe of Russian anarchism, which was so overtaken by events, so unable to rise to their level, despite the fine resources it could count on.

Finally we must ask all anarchists to be willing to discuss calmly, without prejudice and without dogmatism, the experience of the Russian revolution. And we ask them not to adopt and endorse the malicious 'criticisms' (if they deserve that name!) that the bourgeois press of both hemispheres has directed unceasingly against the instigators of the first social revolution. They must not forget that the defeat of a revolution for the success of which men have done all that it was humanly possible to attempt (men who certainly, like all men, are not free of mistakes nor free from blame) would be a terrible disaster for the whole of humanity, a disaster which to a considerable extent could be blamed on those revolutionaries who, by their narrow sectarianism, had helped to divide and demoralise the vanguard of the working-class at the time of greatest danger.

PETROGRAD, 5 JUNE 1921

The need to revise our ideas

After the experience of war and revolution, revolutionary ideology, whether socialist, syndicalist or anarchist, cannot confine itself to the old formulae, any more than we can confine ourselves to the old forms of propaganda and action in the period of large-scale struggles that we have now entered. The bankruptcy of intellectuals and pacifists; the bankruptcy of parliamentary socialist parties; the bankruptcy of bureaucratic syndicalism; and the bankruptcy too of anarchist action—which on the whole was more or less negligible, while certain anarchist militants also lost their lucid understanding of things. Such is the balance-sheet of the war, from a revolutionary point of view. Nonetheless the war verified and tragically confirmed all our predictions. We did not need to see the world in the grip of total madness to know what disasters the old society based on capital and authority was leading its servile masses towards. And so, from the catastrophe in which so many people and organisations were destroyed, the essential ideas emerged strengthened. All the more so since the social revolution, victorious in Russia, temporarily suppressed in central Europe, on the point of setting alight southern Europe—Spain, Italy, the Balkans—has for the last three years been announcing the real power of ideas which so recently were no more than ideas.

Thus not one of the concepts, not one of the words which we used before the war and the revolution has ceased to be necessary for us: on the contrary, a number of those which at that time were only words now refer to *realities*; but there is not a single one of them which can be used in precisely the same way as previously. All the words, we are aware, all the concepts, have in some small way acquired a new meaning. It's an obvious fact. Just consider for one moment the ideas of direct action, of the general strike, of communism, as they were understood in 1914 and in 1920—and you will see how they have evolved!

And then we shall be surprised to see just how difficult it is for men, even the militants who are, after all, at the head of the masses, to recognise such an obvious fact. From a sense of tradition, from routine, from self-interest, from inertia, from an incapacity to distinguish words (the old words) and things, from a sad lack of a sense of reality, there are some who return to the notions of yesteryear and confine themselves to repeating them. There are revolutionaries who, during these magnificent and terrible years, have forgotten nothing and learnt nothing. What is terrible is that in these conditions they can do nothing more than they did in the past.

If we wish to get ourselves out of the stagnation in which the revolutionary movement in various countries is floundering, to draw from it all the active forces it contains, to understand the present moment and to fulfil our task, then I believe that an inescapable duty is presented to the conscience of every militant:

After the experience of the war and the revolution, we must initiate a complete and systematic revision of all our ideas. We must have no fear of laying an irreverent hand on old dogmas which are greatly respected. We must have no fear of stepping off the established paths which seemed so certain—and which led us to fateful dead-ends. But, with a clear knowledge of what we want and of what we are, we must confront reality, examine it calmly and with determination, in order to understand it, to draw our conclusions, and to act.

The new reality in history

The new reality in the social history of our age is that in 1917 the first social—and socialist—revolution took place in Russia. The possessing class was expropriated by the non-possessing class of the exploited. The bourgeois state was smashed. The old social hierarchies collapsed. A new order began to come to birth, whose principles are: collective ownership of the means of production, the requirement that all citizens should work, the elimination of industrial competition within society.

This is a new starting-point in the history of the world. From the moment when the victory of the October revolution on the streets of Petrograd and Moscow (in suffering and poverty, it's true; using violence, it's true; but that was inevitable) laid the foundations of the new society, all events were to acquire a new meaning and a new direction, for the social revolution is not limited to one area. The victory of soviet power in Petrograd and Moscow made the earth shake in Washington, Paris, Tokyo and all the great cities of the world. Countless economic, ideological and moral bonds link people from one end of the world to the other: and the appeal, emanating from Russia, to the deepest interests, to the class interests of the poor, cannot fail to find a formidable resonance. And the revolutionary tide is spreading out from Vladivostok to Berlin, where Liebknecht died; to Munich, where Landauer and Leviné died, to Budapest, to the Ruhr, to Cologne, to Florence, to Turin, to Milan! Might it stop at the banks of the Rhine? It would be madness to think so. Revolutions have never respected frontiers. But they take their own time: if we can be sure that they will not stop before going right round the world, we cannot predict the number of years, or of generations, that they will need to do their work. The great revolution which finished off the Middle Ages and opened up modern times, the Reformation—the affirmation of religious freedom against the corrupt ossified Catholic dogma—devastated Europe for more than a century and by one of its distant repercussions it led to the establishment of the United States of America.[2]

Likewise the victory of the social revolution in Russia is doubtless opening up a revolutionary century. Given the fact of the interdependence of all civilised countries, it is not possible for two different social organisations to exist side by side, in neighbouring countries, the one based on private property, the other on the collective ownership of the means of production. Capitalist imperialism and communism cannot coexist. One must destroy the other. But having reached the absurd final stage of its evolution, culminating as a result of its internal contradictions in war and collapse, capitalist society bears within it the forces which are destined to overthrow it. Cut to pieces by the great slaughter which, precisely, gave birth to the revolution, it stands condemned.

We can say with confidence that social transformation is now only a question of years, or, at the very most, of decades, for the countries of Europe and America. Moreover, the existence of a revolutionary republic creates everywhere psychological conditions which are extremely favourable to the revolt of the masses. By the legendary qualities which it already displays, by the enthusiasm which it inspires, by the example of its heroism and its capacity for suffering, Russia is an inexhaustible source of revolutionary energy. It embodies the future; and the past has no means of resisting it; for guns are plainly no longer able to kill the immense idealism which has been born into the world. Those who fought in the streets of Moscow, of Petrograd, of Yaroslavl and of Vladivostok, those who today are fighting on the various front lines of Soviet Russia, those who are carrying out the humble, melancholy, dangerous—and sometimes immoral—tasks of the revolution, those who are sacrificing themselves to it, are thus working for all humanity and for the whole of the future. When their lives are at stake the fate of humanity is at stake.

The Russian revolution is opening up a new epoch. It is only the first episode of the great revolution which is going to transform the civilised world. Its repercussions will continue for decades, because it is moving towards a radical transformation of the economic and moral conditions of life for the peoples of the world.

This is a truth of vital importance which today seems to be established beyond argument.

A definition of Bolshevism

Such as it is, the social revolution in Russia—and everywhere else that it has begun—is in large part the work of Bolshevism.

Like all historical judgements, this one is in some ways unfair. By formulating it in this way, we seem to be refusing to recognise the enormous and magnificent efforts of all those who, before the time of Bolshevism, *actually practised* revolution: Social Revolutionary propagandists and terrorists, whose courage was unstinting; anarchists and Mensheviks, whom no persecution could stop. Later on, when we rewrite the history of these troubled times, we shall have to do justice to all. But in the meantime, life rewards only those who have succeeded. To survive and to conquer are the greatest virtues. And all the others were found wanting or took the wrong road at the last moment; the Bolsheviks were the ones who *dared*. And that is all that counts.

It is well-known that the Russian word *Bolshevik* simply means *those in the majority*. Within the Marxist Social Democratic party, which contained Plekhanov and Martov, the Bolsheviks were the majority, the advocates of revolutionary intransigence. Until the Russian revolution, they remained in relative obscurity. It was after the fall of Tsarism that they emerged and that their slogans won the enthusiasm of the masses.

In reality, it was a new movement, although its dogged pioneers went back many years. It was the result of the development of socialism to the left. It became prominent at Zimmerwald and at Kienthal.* Reviled and betrayed by the opportunists, by the parliamentarians and the moderates, the socialism which expressed the conscious aspirations of a militant elite, and the still vague aspirations of the masses, became insurrectionary, active, impatient, domineering; and it began to speak a language which hitherto none but the anarchists had spoken.

It is no bad thing to recall the fact. Until the October revolution and for some time afterwards, only the anarchists called themselves communists and declared themselves clearly hostile to state power. The official propagandists of socialism never mentioned the passages in Marx and Engels which dealt with the pernicious nature of the state and the need for it to disappear. Lenin, Zinoviev and Bukharin, by declaring the ideas of communism and the state to be incompatible, were renewing the revolutionary tradition of socialism which, before the remarkable success of their propaganda, had been carried forward only by the various anarchist currents. Before Bolshevism, only the anarchists had rejected bourgeois democracy and patriotism. They alone advocated revolution, that is, the immediate expropriation of the possessing class (see Kropotkin's *The Conquest of Bread*). They

---

* Zimmerwald (September 1915) and Kienthal (April 1916) were international conferences organised by socialists in opposition to World War I. *[Translator's note]*

alone publicly recognised the need to use violence and the principle of terrorism,[3] and there were good reasons why, in the interval between the two revolutions of February and October 1917, Russian Bolsheviks and anarchists co-operated in a fraternal fashion. During the decisive days of July and October, they both initiated action.

For the first time, during the October revolution, words and actions came together. What had so often been spoken of was put into practice. *The unity of thought and action gave Bolshevism its original power;* without entering into doctrinal questions, we can define Bolshevism *as a movement to the left of socialism—which brought it closer to anarchism—inspired by the will to achieve the revolution immediately.*

The will for revolution: the essence of Bolshevism is summed up in these four words.

Lessons of the revolution

Until the present period it was possible to idealise revolution, or, even worse, to talk about it without believing in it. This is no longer possible. It is being carried out before our very eyes in half of Europe, and it is imminent in the other half. On pain of being no more than dreamers and metaphysicians, militants must henceforth envisage it as it really is. It is a great lesson. In the course of a century we had managed to more or less forget the lessons of the French revolution. The Russian revolution brings them back to mind, and provides a vigorous fulfilment of them. So what is a revolution, and what new law does it bring us?

First of all, it is never the epic festival promised us by historians, who in truth were poets rather than historians. It is a storm in which no one is spared, which uproots the strongest, and where the unforeseen triumphs. From the point of view of those who are making it, it is a rough and dangerous task, sometimes a dirty task for which you have to wear knee-length boots and roll up your sleeves, not fearing things that will make you sick. The earth has to be cleansed of the decay of the old world. Filth has to be carried away by the spadeful, and in that filth there is plenty of blood. All the selfishness, the slavishness, the cowardice, the

stupidity which lies at the heart of the human beast will be laid
bare at certain moments. And no splendid sacrifice, no glorious
victory, no stoical idealism in the hearts of the best can eradicate
this display of the weaknesses of past humanity from the minds of
those who have witnessed them.

The revolution is relentless. Relentless in the deprivations
and the trials which it imposes on everyone, which means in the
first instance on the weakest. The first inevitable consequence of
civil war is always the disruption of production. The labour force
is diverted from its peaceful occupations and wasted on the fields
of battle. In the workshops, building sites and factories, where the
old discipline of wage labour has disappeared and the new
mentality has not yet been established, a profound moral disorder
is bound to be rampant. To this are added the disorganisation of
transport, the damage caused by speculation, and the abuses
committed by people fishing in troubled waters. The revolution is
relentless towards the defeated who fall into two groups: on the
one hand defenders of the old regime whom only terror can
finally destroy; on the other hand, disoriented, hesitating,
sentimental revolutionaries. The latter, often as a result of a
narrow party mentality, from an inability to adapt to the terrible
necessities of the moment, from moral scruples in face of the
urgent demands of struggle, sometimes find themselves excluded
from action, still fortunate if ironic fate does not transform them
from being the liberators of yesterday into the counter-
revolutionaries of today.

This concept of revolution as a reality, hard and unrelenting
toil, as opposed to the revolution of myth, is, for the militant, the
first and one of the most important psychological gains of the
years which have just passed. It is such as it is, with all its
formidable consequences, with all the risks it entails and the
sacrifices that it makes necessary, that we must will the revolution
because it is inevitable and necessary; because it is the
precondition for the subsequent evolution of humanity—for the
great rebirth of humankind.

The theoretical experience gained from contemporary
revolutions requires us to accept several other concepts:

1: The Dictatorship of the Proletariat

Revolution implies violence. All violence is dictatorial. All violence imposes the power of a will by breaking resistance. Since the expropriation of the possessing class is at stake, the revolutionary violence which must accomplish this task can only be that of the non-possessing class, that is, of the most advanced minority of the proletariat.

Strengthened and hardened in the revolutionary melting-pots of the great industrial centres, toughened by repeated economic struggles, victim of crises and unemployment, witness of the blatant injustice which allows the same cities to contain the palaces of the parasites and the slums of the workers, the proletariat, whose elite has become clearly aware of its tasks and its duties, is certainly (in contrast to the narrow-minded, conservative peasant, moved by petty interest and often religious) the revolutionary class, and consequently the only class whose violence can put an end to the social war.

I confess that I cannot imagine how anyone could be a revolutionary (other than in a purely individualist fashion) without recognising the necessity for the dictatorship of the proletariat.

There has never been, in history, a revolution without revolutionary dictatorship. Never. Cromwell's England had the dictatorship of the Roundheads. France between 1789 and 1793 had that of the Commune of Paris, then that of the Jacobins. From the day when working-class militants of any tendency, leading the masses, overthrow the power of the bourgeoisie, then even if they are libertarians they will immediately have to organise supplies for the great cities, internal and external defence against the counter-revolution, in short, all the complex mechanisms of modern society. And they cannot rely on the consciousness, the goodwill or the determination of those they have to deal with; for the masses who will follow them or surround them will be warped by the old regime, relatively uncultivated, often unaware, torn by feelings and instincts inherited from the past.

On pain of death, that is, at risk of being immediately put to death by the victory of a reactionary dictatorship, revolutionaries will have to take on the dictatorship without any delay.

2: Soviets or workers' councils

In fact it doesn't matter much which word is used. The soviets in Russia were formed spontaneously during the first days of the February revolution. Elsewhere they may be formed in a different manner. But it nonetheless remains true that, from the very first hours of the social war, councils freely formed by the representatives of the revolutionary workers will be the only bodies to have the moral and material authority necessary to manage production and take the responsibility for action.

This is all the more true because the revolution will necessarily be made against the bourgeois parliament, and in practice this can only be replaced by the principle of workers' councils containing solely the representatives of one class.

3: Terror

There has never been a revolution without terror. In the two great experiences that we know, we can see the very causes that make terror necessary being born and growing. In France from 1791 to 1792, it was the endless conspiring by the nobility, the priests, the speculators and the swindlers within the country; it was the Vendée rising, the revolts at Lyons, Toulon, Marseilles, Mende; it was the émigrés organising foreign intervention from Koblenz and London; it was the armies of the monarchies allied in the counter-revolutionary European coalition crossing the frontiers of the young republic. These causes produced a state of panic among some, a determined, pitiless, furious state of mind among others. A king's head was thrown in the face of Europe, the guillotine was erected on the Place de la République, suspects were arrested by the thousands, and the terrible September massacres were carried out. Nobody willed this sequence of cause and effect; nobody could have evaded its logic.

From 1917 to 1919, in Red Russia, the same causes—the similarity is total—could not fail to produce the same effects. Clearly we are observing a general law of the development of revolutions. We have only to recall the circumstances: revolutionary Russia retreated in face of the need to shed blood for as long as it was possible to retreat. But when the ceaseless plotting within found expression in the Yaroslavl rising, in the murder of Uritsky in Petrograd, in the attempt on Lenin's life in Moscow; when the Ural region, occupied by the Czechoslovaks who were marching on the Volga, became a new Vendée; when the Russian counter-revolutionary émigrés began to organise armed intervention from Paris and London, while their gangs were devastating the Don country; when White Finland had assassinated eleven thousand defeated Communists—then it became necessary to have recourse to Red terror.

It was necessary, on pain of death. For any sign of weakness could have brought about defeat. And defeat meant White terror, a hundred times more terrible than Red terror. In 1871 in Paris in a fortnight, the Versailles forces killed three times as many people as were victims of the Red terror throughout the whole vast territory of Russia in three years of revolution. In Finland, Bavaria and Hungary, the forces of reaction have just shown that they will stop at nothing.

4: *The inevitability of war of revolutionary defence*

Differences in culture, economic development, financial situation, etc, make it very unlikely that revolution will happen completely simultaneously in several large neighbouring countries. The revolution which breaks out and triumphs in one country thus finds itself immediately confronted by an alliance of all the neighbouring states in which the old system still survives. Just as the Europe of the nobles and monarchs allied together against the French republic, so now capitalist Europe (to which, a significant development, the United States and Japan have added their forces) has allied against Communist Soviet Russia. Clemenceau has acted with verve the role once played by Pitt.

It is vital to respond to this necessity for revolutionary defence, as to the necessity for terror and dictatorship, *on pain of death*. For the grim reality of revolutions is that half-measures and half-defeats are not possible, and that victory means *life*, defeat means *death*.

5 : *The necessity of powerful revolutionary organisations*

It was thanks to the remarkable organisation of the Jacobin clubs that revolutionary France successfully resisted the coalition of the European monarchies. As in the case of the Communist party in Russia, the necessities of the revolution had led to the springing up, in Paris and in the provinces, of clubs which, with better organisation, could undoubtedly have held the military and bourgeois reactions in check. Moreover, to hope to defeat the capitalist state without strong and flexible combat organisations, without a whole combat apparatus—publications, economic action, illegal action, terrorism, etc—would be worse than naïve. Revolutionary energy, which by its very nature is multiple and diverse, must be organised, concentrated, coherent and conscious in battle.

The anarchists and the experience of the revolution

These points, I believe, make up the lessons of the Russian revolution. These are the problems which anarchists have an obligation to confront in an open-minded fashion. Otherwise, in the events which are unfolding, they will not play—as anarchists—any significant role, and that will be a miserable abdication of responsibility on their part.

This is an important question. For it does not concern only those who label themselves as 'anarchists'. It is one which concerns all revolutionaries who love liberty, and are imbued with the spirit of free criticism and free investigation which is the basic characteristic of the anarchist psychology: all those who are not dogmatic, all those who believe in the necessity of having a personal conviction, of following their conscience in struggle and trusting nothing but their conscience; all those who believe that the ultimate aim of all revolutionary efforts can only be the achievement of a society of free workers where human individuality could at last be fully established. For those who think and feel in this way, however vaguely, are, whatever label they adopt, anarchists without realising it.

Now, it seems to me that we anarchists must either accept or reject as a whole the set of conditions necessary for the social revolution: dictatorship of the proletariat, principle of soviets, revolutionary terror, defence of the revolution, strong organisations.

Nothing can be subtracted from this whole without the

edifice collapsing. That is how the revolution is. It is a fact. It is not how we dreamed of it, nor what we wanted it to be. Here it is. Are you against it—or with it? The question is posed in this brutal fashion.

For those who put their entire trust in the achievements of education, in the evolution of the masses, and who believe that such education, such evolution can take a libertarian direction within the capitalist system, the question is settled. They expect nothing of violence, they are against the revolution. That means that it will sweep them away despite themselves, and without their trying to understand it. I know that arguments can be made for this point of view. But the error on which it is based seems to me too obvious for it to be worth the effort of refuting it, and this abstentionism in face of the greatest events of history will never appeal either to the masses or to energetic individuals.

So, willy-nilly, most anarchists will be with the revolution. Indeed, everywhere they will be the first to face danger, as they were in Russia. But it is one thing to fight, another to think, to exercise an influence, to enlighten the minds of others. They will be found wanting in this latter task if they do not consciously accept all the necessities of the revolution, though without abandoning their own idealism.

Having advocated for many years class warfare, direct action, the need to use violence, anarchists have no logical reason to reject the dictatorship of the proletariat, a decisive expression of the class struggle, of direct action, of the use of violence; on the contrary, their job is to breathe life into it by infusing it with their spirit, by preventing people misusing words to the prejudice of things, by insisting, for example, that there can be no proletarian dictatorship *without the effective and permanent supervision of the masses* over institutions and people. Doubtless all Communists know this; but their sense of discipline and their habits of centralisation make those of them who are not libertarians less fit to recommend or indeed exercise this supervision.

I do not see how, even from the most intransigent anarchist standpoint, one can make any serious objection to the principle of soviet power. It effectively achieves the minimum of delegation of powers, since members of the soviet remain among their workmates, being elected only for a very short period and liable to be recalled at any moment. And in short, comrades, the soviets will be what you make them!

A number of Russian anarchists have severely criticised the terror, which, of course, nobody accepted light-heartedly. It none the less remains true that they have often resorted to individual terrorism. Can one accept individual terrorism in a time of relative (very relative, admittedly) social peace and yet repudiate the terrorism of the masses in times of civil war? However reluctant we may be to resort to it, can we avoid it being organised and systematically applied? Certainly not.

Now let us pose the question of revolutionary defence. The Russian anarchists, in theory very divided on this question, in practice everywhere resolved it by taking up arms, first of all in the Red Guards, later in the Red army. By forming bands of partisans, they fought against Denikin; they contributed to the defence of Petrograd against Yudenich; they shed their blood on all the fronts of the Soviet Republic. Yet in theory most of them accept only partisan warfare or a volunteer army. It is an ambiguous position. Anyone who agrees to fight may end up winning. Can we defeat the armies of modern imperialism with bands of armed partisans, bands of volunteers? Logic tells us the answer must be no. And experience is conclusive. The necessities of struggle have successively—and victoriously—transformed the Red Guards into a volunteer army, then into a Red army, based on the principle of compulsory service. The anarchist bands of Makhno were able to do no more than survive in the Ukraine during all the invasions which they could not prevent, and even that was possible only because they too resorted to compulsion in order to recruit fighters.

The question of revolutionary organisation is probably the one which would offer anarchists the best reasons for differentiating themselves. Centralisation or federalism? How is it possible to ensure cohesion in action and method, with everything in the perspective of an aim which is often quite remote, and at the same time stimulate the initiative of groups and individuals, and be on one's guard against bureaucracy, against those who claim infallibility, against the dictatorial zeal of committees, against careerism? How is it possible to create a discipline which is not based on passivity? These are questions to which no-one as yet has produced satisfactory answers. Moreover, they are linked to important questions of tactics and principle. The Bolshevik formula of 'a highly centralised party' is open to many criticisms. But if we see this also as merely the expression of an inevitable and necessary reality in the course of the revolution, then all the objections made to the theory will appear to be wholly futile. And such is the case. I shall return to this point a little later on.

The attitude of the Russian anarchists

What was the attitude of the Russian anarchists in face of these facts?

It varied from one extreme to the other, according to the different tendencies.

There were in Russia anarchists who were mortal enemies of the Bolshevik party, but who acted honestly towards it (though with a hint of hostility) or allied with it, often to the extent of actually joining the party.

During the struggle against the collapsing government of Kerensky, anarchists and Bolsheviks pursued parallel actions in a fraternal manner. Likewise the anarchists participated in the July Days and in the decisive battles of October. After October, and for quite a long time, they maintained a formidable autonomy in the large cities: in short, they constituted, inside the great republic that was in process of birth, an armed republic which was badly organised but very turbulent. In Petrograd and in Moscow they had, in palaces which they had occupied, headquarters and actual fortresses bristling with machine-guns. Their general staffs organised searches, arrests, requisitions, without any regulation— and without it being possible to draw a clear line between revolutionary acts and banditry. Likewise the absence of formal organisation made it impossible to distinguish genuine anarchists from those fishing in troubled waters who found it convenient to describe themselves as such. At this point the anarchist press was influential. It had daily papers in Petrograd, in Moscow (*Burevestnik* and *Anarkhiya*) and elsewhere, for example Kronstadt, where for a time the anarchists controlled the soviet whose publication was in fact their publication. Despite many mistakes, despite the absence of a clear programme—a terrible lack at a time when action was necessary and decisions had to be taken every day—they encountered enormous sympathy in the working-class population. They were incapable of taking advantage of this to establish a serious movement, the starting-point for which would have had to be the elaboration of a practical programme. And their widespread agitation faded out for want of a clear ideology, for want of organisation, and as a result of the abuses which turned a great part of the population against the followers of the black flag. It all ended in armed conflict with the Bolsheviks, who resorted to force in order to disarm the anarchist strongholds.

For all those who know what a wealth of energy is contained within the anarchist movement, this is a very bitter page of the history of the Russian revolution. But I can't help wondering whether in the great cities of a revolution under attack from two imperialisms, the existence of an armed force which was not under any supervision or any discipline, even of a moral kind, which obeyed nothing but its own impulses and which necessarily attracted elements who were dubious in every respect, would not, if it had been allowed to continue, have represented a very great danger for the revolution itself. In such a situation, the anarchists themselves would have had to disarm—if necessary, by force—the other anarchists who were thus threatening their life and their achievements.

This conflict struck a very serious blow against the movement. It discredited it, cut off its support and created a gulf between the majority of anarchists and the Communist party. Since then, the movement has merely vegetated, except in the Ukraine, where its experience has been both epic and heart-rending.[4]

At the present time the anarchists have neither press nor organisation, even though there are anarchist militants in nearly every city and every military unit. The differences of opinion among them and the lack of a practical programme for action have excluded them from activity more than any other political reason.

For either they are against the Communist party, and thus pushed towards the counter-revolutionaries and reduced to the same impotence; or they are with it, and since they have no solutions of their own to propose, they have to tail behind it—or join it. However, it is possible to distinguish three tendencies among them:

1. The 'clandestine' or 'underground anarchists', mortal enemies of the Communist dictatorship, which they denounce for its abuses, for the excessive power of its officials, for its centralisation and for the sufferings of the people consequent on the revolution. They have advocated armed struggle against the soviet power and, responding in fact to measures of repression exercised in the Ukraine, they were responsible for the attack on the central committee of the Moscow Communist Party on 25 September 1919, which caused twenty-six injuries and ten deaths, and which provoked unanimous disapproval among the vast majority of anarchists. The organisation which committed this outrage seems to have been entirely destroyed in the struggle it subsequently undertook against the Special Commission for the Suppression of Counter-revolution and Sabotage.

2. Those whom I shall call the Centre, because they occupy an intermediate position between the anti-Communist anarchists and those who are Communists (in the Bolshevik sense of the term). They are by far the majority. The dictatorship, the lack of freedom, abuses of every sort often distress and embitter them. In theory, they criticise the Communist party for its authoritarian conduct, for its principles of absolute centralisation, for its stress on state control, for its intolerance. At first sight their criticisms are very powerful; but as soon as they are examined in any depth, they become empty, since they are not backed up by any indication of a solution.

For example, the statement of principles by the Moscow Union of Anarchists (December 1919) contains, *as its entire political programme*, the few simple lines headed 'In Politics':

We fight for the total emancipation of mankind, not in order to replace the rule of one class by that of another, but in order to destroy all authority, all right of coercion, all laws based on constraint; we wish to replace them by the spontaneous order based on agreements freely entered into.

The present state ruled by a class—the forced association of individuals and groupings—must be replaced by the free association of individual persons.

We fight for the destruction of all state-imposed frontiers and boundaries. We declare that the whole earth must belong to all men and to all peoples!

This is certainly a splendid statement which very clearly sums up the ideal of *all Communists* (including those who have never borne any name other than that of Bolsheviks). But how can this ideal be achieved, how can we set to work on it straightaway, in 1920, in the context of present events? Merely to invoke the ideal in this way means founding propaganda on utopianism. I am obliged to agree that Bukharin did much better—though less poetically—in his *ABC of Communism*, where he outlined the theory of the withering away of the state and of all authority by means of the normal functioning of communist economic institutions.

This critical utopian position, made very weak by the fact that those who defend it now advocate no practical action, is that of the Anarchist Youth Federation, of the Moscow Union and of most of the small groups.

The Ukrainian Anarchist Confederation of the *Nabat* (Alarm Bell) is also situated in the centre, with more practical sense and a much stronger theory, thanks to a very valuable activist, Voline (Eichenbaum). A number of the *Nabat* comrades accept the dictatorship of the working-class, but deny the need for a defined period of transition between capitalism and communism. The revolution cannot stop; it must continue until the establishment of complete communism which can only be libertarian. Any attempt to found a 'communist state' which is halfway between the old system and the new society is in their eyes pernicious. The revolution must be on a worldwide scale. The creative forces of the masses will play the vital role in it. Everything comes from the masses, and all that is needed is constantly to appeal to them. The masses organise themselves into local soviets which will spontaneously federate and form militias or more precisely groups of insurgents (I am translating the Russian word *povstantsi*) which have the potential of becoming a volunteer army. This means that *Nabat* is intransigently opposed to any centralisation *from above* and to military service imposed by a central authority. In the Ukraine this ideology has encountered great success. If it had not come up against the Marxist Communism of the Great Russians, it seems, according to well-informed witnesses, that it might have been able to produce positive results, that is, a distinctly original orientation for the social revolution in the Ukraine. The *Nabat* confederation still enjoys a certain prestige among anarchists throughout Russia because of the epic aspects of the struggle in the Ukraine. But in reality it has only a local significance and value.

3. The 'Soviet' anarchists who believe that at the present time they have a duty to work with the Bolshevik Communist party and even to go over to it completely. Indeed, numerous comrades have joined the party, believing that the present time was not one for philosophical reservations, and that its programme was the only practical and feasible one to safeguard the gains of the October revolution. Without joining the party, the comrades of the anarcho-syndicalist group *Golos Truda* (Moscow and Petrograd) have in practice made common cause with it, going so far as to approve of the militarisation of labour (Grossman-Roshchin, late 1919).

They recognise, admittedly in rather confused terms, the need for a revolutionary dictatorship during the transition period, but not the necessity for a political party.

At the same time as this group we should mention that of the anarchist-universalists, recently founded in Moscow, which accepts centralisation with all its logic in a revolutionary period. 'On all tactical questions,' one of its militants told me in 1920, 'we are in agreement with the Bolsheviks.' [5]

To sum up, the insignificance of the anarchist influence, despite the role played by anarchist militants in all the revolutionary struggles, is striking throughout Russia, with the exception of the Ukraine. In my view this can be explained by the following factors:

First of all by the fact that Bolshevism, at least in its earlier phases of destruction and struggle, is working for future anarchy, of which it has absorbed those principles which are feasible at present; secondly, by the fact that to a great extent Bolshevism is no more than the (inevitable) result of the action of laws which govern the development of any revolution (so that no room is left for alternative methods); finally, to a much lesser extent, because of the attachment to tradition on the part of anarchists who have failed to face up to events in a practical fashion. Even in Russia most of them have not yet taken a clear position in face of the dictatorship of the proletariat.

Centralisation and Jacobinism

Thus the revolution develops by virtue of rigorous laws whose consequences are not open to discussion. We have to counteract them and modify them within the limits of our powers, and our criticism may be usefully exercised in this direction. But such criticism must not make us lose sight of the fact that we are often dealing with unchangeable necessities—that it is a question of the internal logic of any revolution and that, as a result, it would be absurd to put the blame for particular facts (however deplorable) on the wishes of a group of men, on a doctrine or on a party. Rather than being moulded by men, doctrines and parties, the revolution moulds them. Only those who conform to its necessities are granted the appearance of being superior to events; the others are cast aside or broken. That is doubtless why the anarchists, unskilled in adapting themselves to new circumstances, have generally been carried away by the storm—and sacrificed; while the Marxists, being more prudent realists, bravely adapted to the necessities of the hour. Their supreme merit in so doing was never to lose sight of the final goal.

The suppression of so-called freedoms; dictatorship backed up if necessary by terror; the creation of an army; the centralisation for war purposes of industry, food supplies and administration (whence state control and bureaucracy); and finally, the dictatorship of *a party*. In this fearsome chain of necessities, there is not a single link which is not rigorously conditioned by the one that precedes it and which does not in turn condition the one that follows it.

In 1917-1920 in Russia, as in 1789-1797 in France, these

were the consequences of a struggle to the death by a
revolutionary minority against a reactionary minority;
consequences—of the disintegration of the old society, of the
crisis of industry, of famine, of the breakdown of the moral
incentives which held individual egoisms in check, of the clash of
enthusiasms and fanaticisms—in short, of the class war, at home
and on an international scale, transforming the whole country into
an entrenched camp where, in the last resort, there is no longer
any law except martial law.

In an article called 'Anarchist criticism and the necessities of
the revolution'* I have examined the main aspects of these
questions at some length. As I do not believe it is necessary to
develop further an argument of which the main features have
already been adequately set out, I shall confine myself to a few
observations on centralisation and the action of the Communist
party.

The anarchist tradition is, with good reason, one of
decentralisation. It fights centralisation in the name of individual
initiative. It presents federalism as an alternative. All well and
good. But today can we be satisfied with the traditions of the Jura
Federation?† Should we not rather discriminate, probe more
deeply, state more precisely. Indeed we should—and perhaps it is
not very difficult. The pernicious form of centralisation, that
which kills initiative, is *authoritarian centralisation*. For it is self-
evident that even in the most libertarian communist society, at
least certain industries (let us say by way of example) must be run
on the basis of a single plan, according to an overall picture and on
the basis of precise statistics, etc. It is even more accurate to say
that industry as a whole will have to have, over and above the
millions of brains which give it life, a *single brain*. But the function
of this *centre* will be to manage on the basis of science and not of
authority; it will impose itself because it will be the beneficial
result of the efforts of all the bodies involved in production and

---

* This is probably one of the articles published by Serge in *Le Libertaire*
in 1919-21.

† French Swiss section of the First International, under the influence of
Bakunin. *[Translator's notes]*

not because it is feared; it will stimulate, enlighten, co-ordinate and use the free initiatives of autonomous groups and of individuals which it will not aspire to dominate by means of coercion. In short, what is pernicious in the principle of centralisation as it understood at the present time is the authoritarian spirit. If this spirit is set aside, all that remains is *co-ordination*. The future will doubtless eliminate, although not without great struggles, the authoritarian spirit, the last trace of the spirit of exploitation. To aspire towards this, in revolutionary periods, anarchists can no longer deny the need for a certain degree of centralisation, and nonetheless they have a contribution to make, a contribution that they alone can make. What they must say is as follows:

Centralisation, agreed. But not of an authoritarian type. We may have recourse to the latter *from necessity, but never from principle*. The only revolutionary form of organisation is: *free association, federation, co-ordination*. It does not exclude the centralisation of skills and information; it excludes only the centralisation of power, that is, of arbitrariness, of coercion, of abuse. It must spring from the masses and not be sent down to them in order to control them.

In this respect, we must hope that in more culturally advanced countries, where the masses have more experience of organisation and self-discipline, the bitter experiences of Russia will not be repeated. In Russia the dictatorship of the proletariat had to apply an authoritarian centralisation which became ever fuller. We may and should deplore this. Unfortunately I do not believe it could have been avoided. The lack of organisation, the generally low level of culture of the Russian people, the shortage of men, the great quantity of mistakes and abuses, the immense danger—all these compelled the revolution increasingly to monopolise power in the hands of its most experienced leaders. We have seen this experience developing before our very eyes. The 'local autonomous powers' committed so many mistakes— and sometimes worse than mistakes—that the transfer of authority to the capital produced a sigh of relief.

This question is closely linked to that of revolutionary organisation before and during the period of the decisive struggles. The considerations set out above are relevant to this. But historical experience and logic lead us here to two conclusions as to the *inevitability of Jacobinism*. Excellent revolutionaries claim that 'the dictatorship of the proletariat must not be that of a party', and it is difficult not to agree with them immediately, if we are looking at what should, that is at what *ought to*, be the case. Perhaps, in other historical conjunctures, the various ideological currents of the revolutionary movement will achieve a certain balance, which is of course wholly desirable for the subsequent development of the new society. But it seems doubtful. For it appears that by force of circumstances one group is obliged to impose itself on the others and to go ahead of them, breaking them if necessary, in order then to exercise an exclusive dictatorship. That was the experience of the Jacobins of the Mountain who crushed first the Girondins and then the Commune. That was the experience of the Bolsheviks, obliged to overcome in turn the Mensheviks, the Social Revolutionaries and the anarchists. Any other organisation—even if it had been libertarian—would have had to do the same in their situation. For at such moments, the opposition, whatever it may be, becomes in practice the ally of the external counter-revolution; for intolerance is raised to its highest pitch by the very development of revolutionary psychology.

In certain countries, the trade unions—and as a result the revolutionary syndicalist minority—seem destined to play an absolutely decisive role in the coming revolutionary crises. If one day they lay hold of the means of production, they will have to break the resistance of the reformist elements; and the minority taking the initiative, the conscious minority leading the movement, will have to organise itself to exercise a moral control over the unions themselves, in order to purge them and to thwart any plots: for example, if the minority in question is *libertarian*, it will have no option but to fight (and it will not always be able to choose what means to use) against the plots of the *authoritarians!!!* The Russian Communists shrank from the necessity of accepting exclusive power until the day when the attempt by the Left Social Revolutionaries to seize power by force (the Moscow insurrection of 7-8 July 1918) compelled them to do so. Until that date both parties held power. On 7 July 1918 the Social Revolutionaries rose up, and took over the postal and telegraphic services in order to let the country know that 'henceforth they would rule on their own'; cannon were fired at the Kremlin, where the People's Commissars were resident. They were defeated; and then it was the Bolsheviks who ruled alone. It is highly dubious whether parties and groupings in other countries will, in similar circumstances, be better able to resist the temptation to control events on their own, and thus behave more moderately. For who is not capable of risking everything in order to achieve their ideal in full? The formation of a Jacobin party and the exclusivity of the dictatorship do not therefore appear inevitable; and everything henceforth depends on the ideas which inspire it, on the men who apply these ideas, and on the reality of control by the masses.

The pitiless logic of history seems hitherto to have left very little scope for the libertarian spirit in revolutions. This is because human freedom, which is the product of culture and of the raising of the level of consciousness, cannot be established by violence; precisely the revolution is necessary to win—by force of arms—from the old world of oppression and exploitation the possibility of an evolution that hopefully will be peaceful and which will lead us to spontaneous order, to the free association of free workers, to anarchy.

So it is all the more important, throughout all these struggles, to preserve the *libertarian spirit.* And in this respect we may nourish high hopes. The countries which will now be the next to take the revolutionary road will no longer have to fear the protracted ordeals of the Russian revolution, the assault of two imperialisms, stretched out for years, the blockade and all the distress it produced; from the very first hour they will have a powerful ally in the Russian revolution which has taken on their behalf the first and the most difficult steps.

The revolution is a sacrifice to the future

These are indeed 'harsh truths'. But such is the reality of revolutions. It really is too easy to label oneself a revolutionary without taking the trouble to study the historical experience of more than a century. In the eyes of the anarchist in particular, the spectacle of revolutions no longer has anything idyllic about it.

To all that is terrible in the words 'civil war', 'dictatorship', 'intolerance', 'terror', must be added the unleashing of anti-social instincts, the almost total cessation of scientific and artistic production, an apparent regression in morality, abuses of all sorts; just think of the victims, victims too many to count.

But others have said it before us: the more violent the storm, the shorter it will be. How many are the victims of the social peace that exists under capitalism? By poverty, by social diseases (tuberculosis, syphilis, alcoholism, crime, prostitution), by economic and moral crises, how many lives does it sacrifice (imperceptibly, for we are so used to living in a poisoned atmosphere) every single day to the domination of the rich? As for wars, an inevitable consequence of the capitalist system, how many victims do they create? Certain single days of slaughter in the recent war may have cost humanity more lives than were lost by three years of revolution in a country of 140 million inhabitants.

Every revolution is a sacrifice of the present to the future. What is at stake is the future of humanity. Made necessary by the previous economic and psychological evolution, this sacrifice conditions future progress. And it would be wholly accurate to say that it does not add to the total of the victims of what is called order, of what is in reality domination, both hypocritical and violent, by the powers of conservatism. For none of those who fall on the road of revolution—none, except a few privileged people who belong to the ruling class—would have been spared by poverty, by war, by the calamities of the capitalist order.

The danger of state socialism

From what has gone before, one conclusion stands out. The revolution is leading us irresistibly towards state socialism (state capitalism).

Determined opponents of state power, the Russian Bolshevik Communists have nonetheless taken their decision in this situation. They are founding a state. They have an army, a police, a judicial system, a diplomatic service, ambassadors. And they are seeking to find the most effective means of destroying the state. The Communist plan provides for it to *wither away* rapidly. This clear awareness of the aim, preserved throughout the most varied adaptations to the different aspects of the struggle, indicates *strength* and *will*.

But it obliges us to ask the most important question. Can the state die a natural death, to be replaced by free associations of producers? Lenin asserts it *(State and revolution)*; Bukharin *(The ABC of Communism)* attempts to prove it by showing how the normal functioning of the soviet regime gradually abolishes the old apparatus of compulsion that is known as the state by appealing to the energy of the masses. The full achievement of the Bolshevik Communist programme would lead us to libertarian communism, to anarchy.

The danger of state communism—even when conceived of and carried out with such a programme—is that the state may obstinately persist in surviving. If we work on the basis of the historical method, that seems in fact to be probable. Never have we seen an authority *voluntarily disappear*. The socialist state, which has become omnipotent through the fusion of political and economic power, served by a bureaucracy which will not hesitate to attribute privileges to itself and to defend them, will not disappear of its own accord. The interests clustered around it will be too strong. In order to uproot and destroy it, the Communists themselves may need to resort to profoundly revolutionary activity which will be long and difficult. Any revolutionary government is, by its very nature, conservative and hence reactionary. Power exerts on those who exercise it a pernicious influence, which is often expressed in the form of deplorable professional deformations. It has an irresistible attraction for profiteers, careerist politicians, born authoritarians (a type of exploiter on the psychological level) and crooks. This mob of essentially counter-revolutionary elements automatically excludes from power free spirits, proud and simple characters, men who are disgusted by plotting and careerism. This corruption of power could be observed in France under the Directory and the Consulate.[†] Russian militants know how hard it is to fight it.

---

* The Directory (1795-99) and Consulate (1799-1804) were the French governments between the fall of the Jacobins and Napoleon's Empire. *[Translator's note]*

In short, it constitutes the great internal danger of the revolution. State communism, which has indisputable advantages over the chaos of capitalist production, would also run the risk of crystallising in the same way, if the Communists did not take precautions against it. Now among the Communists some are temperamentally inclined to underestimate the danger; others let themselves be charmed by the perquisites of power; it will be the task of libertarian Communists to recall by their criticisms and by their actions that at all costs the workers' state must be prevented from crystallising.

The important thing is that the Communist state, straight after the revolution, should fulfil its task, which is to ensure the maximum welfare and leisure to all citizens. By suppressing the idleness and the parasitism of the rich, by rationally reorganising production and the distribution of goods—under the especially rigorous supervision of the masses—it will be relatively easy for it to achieve this result. Now, prosperity and leisure condition freedom and libertarian education. And in this way state communism, even if it diverges from its revolutionary and progressive direction, will nonetheless have achieved the necessary preconditions for a subsequent development which will enable it to be destroyed and replaced by a stateless communism, the free association of producers.

The state and production

Thus as far as the old question of state control, so often disputed between socialists and anarchists, is concerned, the experience of the social revolution in Russia leads us to a twofold conclusion: first of all the necessity of taking hold of the state, a powerful apparatus of coercion; and secondly the necessity of defending ourselves against it, of relentlessly working for its destruction, perhaps at the price of a long and laborious struggle.

Four years have already elapsed since the great revolution of modern times. Today it seems to me to be possible to formulate, at least approximately, a new conclusion about the role and the mission of the state as a tool of revolutionary dictatorship in a transitional period.

It would be a mistake to attribute the formation in Russia of

a workers' and peasants' state to the conscious intentions of
Marxist Jacobins—although Marxist notions of centralisation and
the Jacobin spirit formed in the struggle between parties are
certainly not foreign to it. But it seems to me to be quite obvious
that any other revolutionary tendency or grouping would, in the
same historical conjuncture, have acted very similarly to the
Russian Bolsheviks. The formation of the Red army, the transition
from voluntary to compulsory military service, courts, centralised
administration—these were all deplorable but inevitable devices to
wage war against the enemies without and within (the latter took
many forms, for hunger, ignorance and error are also enemies
within); even if one were a libertarian, one faced the task of
fighting against modern armies without having a modern army of
one's own. The function creates the organ: the army is the product
of war. Discipline, centralised command, even a single command
covering several fronts, centralisation of the enormous apparatus of
supplies, relief and transport at the rear—then nationalisation,
militarisation of war industries, which in modern warfare means
virtually all industries; everything is interconnected and rigorously
necessary in this field. Moreover, against the enemy within, the
apparatus of control, coercion and terror, at the summit of which,
whether we like it or not, is always the revolutionary tribunal and
the Lord Low Executioner of class justice (after all, our
revolutionary justice is not more beautiful than *theirs!*) Here we
have the two faces of the revolutionary state, the instrument of
domination of one class over another, in these circumstances
turned against the bourgeois class *in order to destroy it* as a class.

In all this the role of the state is very clear: to kill. Kill the
enemy without, by making war. Kill the enemy within by
repression, passing sentence and instituting terror. The state is a
weapon, an instrument of death, *a killing machine.*

Hence its inability to manage production. To kill and to
oblige men to get themselves killed, we need constraint, harshness,
violence which crushes masses and individuals, violence which
crushes consciousness. To produce—and above all to produce
during great crises, during periods of moral confusion, of privation
and danger, we need on the contrary interest, initiative, dedication
(or at the very least goodwill), the willing self-discipline of the

producer. The application of methods of constraint to production, the attempts at the militarisation of labour in Russia (1919-1920) have, I think, adequately demonstrated that they could only be used as an expedient in the most difficult times, but that under no circumstances can they contribute to a lasting restoration of production.

One of the misfortunes of Red Russia has precisely been that it has been unable to avoid the almost total nationalisation of production. The programme of the Bolshevik Communist party provides for the transfer of production to the trade unions. But at the time of the October revolution, there were hardly any syndicalists in Russia, and there were no organisations of producers to take over production. Of necessity the state which was conducting the armed defence of the revolution had to take over industry—and not without invoking in its support a host of good reasons. A whole quite specific ideology was to flow from this circumstance, as a result of which production has greatly suffered. So it will easily be understood that, in the autumn and winter of 1920, the whole of Communist Russia took a passionate interest in the debate about the role of the trade unions in production. All the tendencies and all the leaders of the revolution were, in fact, agreed in desiring to see this role as essential; but the embryonic state of the unions, the scarcity of militants in a proletariat which was completely exhausted by the civil war, and almost all of whose energies had been absorbed by the party, did not allow a conclusive answer to be given to the question.

The confusion between the internal and external defence of the revolution and the organisation of production, resulting from the subordination of the creative apparatus (industry) to the destructive and murderous apparatus (the state) seems to me today to be as serious in the field of ideas as in the field of facts.

This is not wholly avoidable. In a period of revolution, it is sometimes much more important to kill than to produce. In all periods people produce in order to live. When a revolution is being made, they more or less stop producing in order to fight. So it is in the very logic of the facts that the revolutionary state should have a strong tendency to subordinate everything to itself. However, the ideal would be for the system of production to be taken out of the hands of the possessing classes and given to the producers, thus becoming the only centre of gravity which would subordinate the defence apparatus to itself and require obedience from it. But reality will always be a compromise between the ideal and the necessary.

In countries other than Russia, where there is already a well established industrial base, together with a large skilled proletariat, powerfully organised and prepared by long years of industrial struggle for the expropriation of the wealthy classes, the organisations of producers, the trade unions, will doubtless have a key role to play in the revolution. Even if they fail to exercise this role in full, they will certainly participate for a long time in the dictatorship of the proletariat. The only theoretical conception which, in my view, needs to be formulated as of now is that it will be necessary, on pain of making the most painful and dangerous mistakes, to establish a very clear notion of the historical mission of the state, and not to confuse two things which are absolutely distinct, although closely interrelated at certain points in time, namely war and production. The producers can make war, and that is what happens in the social war: the army, the police and the bureaucracies which they maintain can neither produce nor effectively ensure that production takes place.

I recognise the inadequacy of this insight, among many others. When the overall lessons of the Russian revolution are drawn, I am sure that the relations between the state and production will be studied at great length—and that the conclusion will hardly be in favour of the nationalisation of production. The revolutionary slogan of the future, I believe, should rather be: Production to the producers, that is, to the trade unions.

From a different point of view, moreover, we shall find ourselves even in this case confronted with state control within the organisations of production. With its bureaucratic and administrative habits, with its staff of full-time officials and its own legal processes, a union like the CGT* could very well itself become a sort of state in a real sense. It is a complex problem. But

---

* Confédération Générale du Travail - the main French trade union body, founded 1895. [*Translator's note*]

even with this terrible deformation, an industrial confederation of unions would be better equipped to organise production than the political and military mechanism of the bourgeoisie, taken from it and turned back against it.

The great confirmations of anarchism

As soon as it becomes possible for revolutionaries to cast an eye over the road they have travelled so far and to draw up a balance-sheet of the struggle, all critical minds will have to accept certain conclusions which will already be familiar to anarchists. Already today there are certain ones which seem to be beyond doubt. They are:

• *The deadly harmful nature of authority;*

• *The harmful nature of state control and of authoritarian centralisation.*

(These are the cause of the doubtless inevitable and necessary evils which arise in a period of social transformation; evils which we must, to a very large extent, learn to accept, but which are none the less evils, something which should not be forgotten.)

It will be observed that here we have, quite simply, the refutation in practice of the principles of authority, that is, one of the essential postulates of the anarchist philosophy.

The revolutionary movement is never more seriously put to the test than by the seizure of power. From the very day after it takes place, no one who is observing things closely can deny that the exercise of authority is the worst cause of economic and psychological corruption, whether for parties, for groups or for individuals.

Economic corruption, since the possession of power is itself a privilege, which immediately creates numerous categories of privileged persons. It encourages the sacrifice of economic considerations to political considerations (the preservation and reinforcement of power). This in turn can lead to the most undesirable consequences.

Psychological corruption, since authority produces a professional deformation in whoever exercises it, something which is all the more rapid and marked if we are dealing with a character

which is less resolute, with a way of thinking which is less
cultivated and libertarian. In the one who commands, it arouses
arrogance, scorn for the personality of others, and, in times of
social war, brutality and general contempt for human life; in the
one who has to obey, it produces servility, hypocrisy, dishonesty
or, in the best case—all things considered!—the behaviour of a
robot. In such a way does authority corrupt. I would venture to
claim that virtually nobody escapes its depraving effects. That is
why I think I can state it as axiomatic that *the exercise of authority is
one of the most pernicious forms of the exploitation of man by man.* For
whoever carries out the will of another is exploited by another.
And in such a matter, use is inseparable from abuse. One cannot
say where one begins and the other ends. In the everyday practice
of a revolution, authority is generally the exercise of arbitrary
power, and abuses, great and small, become so numerous that it
would be childish to try and consider them in isolation. It is a
terrifying and heart-breaking sight to see how the exercise of
power, even if it is short-lived, even if it is of minimal extent, can
transform anybody at all into a petty tyrant. The obsession with
commanding, prescribing, decreeing, ordering and bullying,
especially when it wins over the uncultivated masses, has been one
of the major causes of the cruelties and of the mistakes of the
Russian revolution. This is, moreover, a very old experience. It is
only necessary to reread the history of the Jacobin dictatorship,
which in this respect is much more instructive than the history of
the present revolution. To prove it one would simply have to
name some of the proconsuls of the Convention.*

This is not the time to make an all too facile criticism of
state socialism and authoritarian centralisation which, by
paralysing initiative, squander an enormous quantity of energy
and create stagnation. The present experience of revolutionary
Russia reveals an energetic and innovative minority which is
compelled to make up for the deficiencies in the education of the
backward masses by the use of compulsion. In this situation it is
probable that no other minority, no minority guided by different

---

* Revolutionary assembly which governed France 1792-95.
[Translator's note]

principles, could have done anything different, and certainly nobody would have done any better. But from its immense efforts we can already draw one conclusion: namely, that those who exercise power can in reality achieve only very few things by means of power. In the successes of soviet Russia (military victories, moral victories and even relative economic victories, since despite everything it has survived) very little credit accrues to authority. Many things have been done despite it, and even when constraint has played a role, almost everything was achieved only as a result of revolutionary idealism, of the action of new interests and of a mass of social factors where coercion scarcely enters into the question. On the contrary, coercion sometimes reveals itself to be virtually impotent. The death penalty used to combat banditry has not succeeded in stamping it out to this very day. The soviet state is not preserved by its apparatus of compulsion, but by its apparatus of agitation and propaganda, and above all because it is the most basic expression of proletarian interests.

I believe violence is necessary to disentangle historical situations and to carry through an evolution which has been blocked by outdated institutions. It destroys the harmful forces of a past which has outlived its usefulness. It kills. It thus opens up vast new possibilities for life. But it creates nothing; it is powerless to give birth to an idea or a creation. And what is dangerous is the fact that it gives birth to a great illusion. For men are prone to nourish illusions about their own capacities, and to believe that they can construct with the same victorious daring that they used for destruction.

But this is not the case. The new society can be built only through knowledge, the spirit of organisation and the unceasing development of the consciousness of the masses and of individuals. The guns and bayonets of the Red army, the decrees and measures of compulsion introduced by the dictatorship of the proletariat— these will kill the old regime and defend the new communist society against attempts to strangle it; but then they must make way for education, propaganda, the initiative of the masses and the organising spirit of leading elements.

The role of anarchists in the communist movement

Within the revolutionary movement, the anarchists represent the spirit of freedom, the critical spirit, individualism, the unending quest—in short, a temperament and a way of approaching life.

They are without doubt revolutionaries.

Is it possible for them, when confronted with the experience of a contemporary revolution, to preserve the standpoint of the old utopianism? Can they carry on confining themselves to pushing the old liberal ideas—which even the bourgeoisie pay hypocritical lip-service to—to their logical conclusion?

No.

And this 'No' is not just my personal opinion. To these questions, the experience of the last few years answers as follows:

If the anarchists fail to adopt a clear and distinct position towards the revolution, and that means all the necessities of the revolution; if they do not unhesitatingly and everywhere align themselves with the revolution, whatever sacrifices it may impose on them (and I am well aware that concessions of principle made in the face of harsh reality are very great sacrifices), then they will be worthless. They will play no role. Some will confine themselves to tailing behind the more determined Communists at a greater or lesser distance. The others—alas! for such is the irony of fate—will find themselves following in the footsteps of reaction.[6]

They will not be able to carry out their task, and to exercise an influence unless, as revolutionaries, they accept their role without hiding from themselves any of the consequences of their position.

If they follow this course, they will become Communists who, in the major episodes of the revolutionary struggle, will necessarily act like all true communists and hand in hand with them. But unlike many others, they will strive throughout these battles to preserve the spirit of liberty, which will give them a greater critical spirit and a clearer awareness of their long-term goals. Within the Communist movement their clear-sightedness will make them the enemies of the ambitious, of budding political careerists and commissars, of formalists, party dogmatists and intriguers. In other words, by their very presence within the organisations, they make a substantial contribution to driving away the self-seekers.

In tactical and theoretical questions their role will be to fight the illusions of power, to foresee and forestall the crystallisation of the workers' state as it has emerged from war and revolution, everywhere and always to encourage the initiative of individuals and of the masses, to recall to those who might forget it that the dictatorship is a weapon, a means, an expedient, a *necessary evil*—but never an aim or a final goal.

The pressure of reaction which is probably most to be feared after a victorious revolution is *reaction in behaviour*, which is expressed almost imperceptibly by a process in which some militants get absorbed into bourgeois practices, as they are decidedly corrupted by power, through an instinctive return to old routines, especially to those of private life. Anarchist philosophy, which appeals to individuals, imposes on them attitudes in their private life and their inner life, proposes a morality, which is something that Marxism, a theory of class struggle, does not do to such a great extent. Armed with the spirit of free enquiry, more liberated than anyone else from bourgeois prejudices with regard to the family, honour, propriety, love, from worrying about 'what people will say' and 'what is expected', militants who see anarchism as 'an individual way of life and activity', in the well-chosen phrase of some of the French comrades, will resist reaction in behaviour with their common sense and their courage in setting an example. While others become officers, functionaries, judges, sometimes joining the privileged elite, they will remain simply men, free workers, who can perform in a stoical fashion all the tasks that are necessary to plough up the old land, but who will never be intoxicated by rhetoric, or by success, or by the lure of profitable careers.

Will they actually join the Communist organisations, or will they organise themselves alongside them so as to co-operate fraternally with them against the common enemy? I am not even going to ask this question, which seems to me to be a secondary one. Circumstances will decide. In practice, the only thing which can impede the agreement of all revolutionaries in common action is the narrow-mindedness of those who see any ideas different from their own as being harmful. The vital thing for anarchists is that they should not belong to this group.

The future

When the revolution is victorious and the country is at peace, the dictatorship of the proletariat and the state will disappear, and as society organises itself more consciously, some people will doubtless feel satisfied. Yet it is necessary always to go forward, unceasingly for ever. Towards what?

'Towards greater material well-being', the masses will reply, not without good reason. But at this juncture the role of the anarchists will be decisive. In all fields of social activity, it will fall to them to bring their answer to this question:

'Towards greater freedom. Towards the fullest development of the human personality.'

Conservative or reactionary tendencies will also appear then. Then, as now, philistines will exist in great numbers. Stupidity, petty egoism and vanity will continue their activity as they have always done. Authority will struggle to survive, thus blocking the way to true life.

So we shall need anarchists in order to go forward, to stimulate the endless quest of the best and the bravest, to ensure the defence of the individual against various intolerant or tyrannical collectivities, to pursue in behaviour and in thought the never-ending revolutionary action which generates all human progress.

Victor Serge
PETROGRAD, JULY-AUGUST 1920

NOTES

1 I owe this excellent term to comrade Amédée Dunois, who in his study *Marxism and Freedom* prefers it to 'historical materialism'.

2 The French revolution took half a century to conquer minds—after having conquered Europe by force of arms—and was rekindled from 1848 in the form of egalitarian, libertarian and fraternal socialism.

3 Few books are so useful in understanding the terrible necessities of the Russian revolution as Kropotkin's *The Great French Revolution*.

4 Epic by the heroism of the anarchist 'partisans', who, armed with spears and clubs, began their insurrectional movement under the German occupation, and who later struck a mortal blow against Denikin by cutting off his communications and destroying his reserves. They could not be subjugated, even though they had no munitions factories, no reserves of arms, no organisation of supplies, no medical services or doctors, though the territory was ravaged by epidemics. Heart-rending because of the anti-Semitic abuses which the militants who took part in the movement were not able to prevent, because of banditry, because of the ferocity of insurgents who ceased to be revolutionaries and became no more than outlaws.

5 Today—June 1921—there are in Moscow two anarcho-syndicalist groups, who can basically be distinguished as left and right; likewise there are two anarchist-universalist groups.

6 Unfortunately this is not just a possibility; it is already a fact. In Monsieur Jouhaux's *La Bataille* Christian Cornelissen and Jean Grave have written articles on Soviet Russia which Albert Thomas and Kautsky would not have repudiated. Charles Malato recently wrote in *France Libre*, the paper of the social patriots dear to the heart of Marshal Pilsudski, a similar article entitled 'On a New Religion'. And there are other examples (1920).

Further reading

For those who want to know more of Serge's writings on the
Russian Revolution and its aftermath there is a considerable
amount of material available in English.

For an account of Serge's life and political evolution the best
starting-point is his *Memoirs of a Revolutionary 1901-1941* (New
York, 1984). All his novels are well worth reading. *Conquered City*
(New York, 1978) portrays Petrograd at roughly the same time as
these pamphlets, while *The Case of Comrade Tulayev* (London,
1993) is perhaps his most striking attack on Stalinism.
Year One of the Russian Revolution (London, 1992) describes the
period immediately preceding that covered in these pamphlets;
Russia Twenty Years After (New Jersey 1996 - also known as *Destiny
of a Revolution*) presents a critique of Stalinism.

The Serge-Trotsky Papers (edited David Cotterill, London, 1994)
traces Serge's complex relations with Trotsky and Trotskyism;
Victor Serge - The Century of the Unexpected (issue 5/3 of
Revolutionary History, 1994) contains a number of important texts
by and about Serge, notably his 1925 essay on Lenin and his 1927
articles on the Chinese revolution.

For a comprehensive bibliography of Serge's writings see Bill
Marshall, *Victor Serge: The Uses of Dissent* (Oxford, 1992).

Glossary

PEOPLE

Antselovich, Naum Markovich (1888-1952); joined Communist
Party 1905; exiled after 1912; organised Red Guard in Petrograd;
Central Committee member from 1938; deputy trade minister
from 1945.

Avrov, Dmitrii Nikolaevich (1890-1922); captain in Tsarist army in
World War I; joined Red Army and Communist Party 1918; took
part in suppression of Kronstadt 1921.

Bulak-Balakhovich, Stanislav Nikodimovich (1883-1940); officer in
World War I; joined Red Army February 1918; defected to
Whites November 1918; fought against soviet forces till
November 1920; then went to Poland; assassinated in Warsaw.

Borghi, Armando (1882-1968); Italian anarchist from 1897;
secretary of the Unione Sindacale Italiana (a syndicalist split from
the General Confederation of Labour); interned 1916-18 for anti-
war activity; visited Russia 1920, but hostile to Communist
International and Red International of Labour Unions; left Italy
1922, in USA 1926-45; returned to Italy 1945, active as anarchist;
in 1960s defended Cuban revolution.

Bukharin, Nikolai (1888-1938); Bolshevik from 1906; in exile
1910-17; opposed Brest-Litovsk as 'left communist'; became
editor of *Pravda;* supported Stalin against left 1923-28; then
dropped by Stalin and removed from all positions; capitulated to
Stalin 1933; became editor of *Izvestia;* executed in 1938.

Churchill, Winston (1874-1975); Tory MP 1900, defected to
Liberals; Minister of Munitions 1917, Secretary of State for War
1919-21; defected back to Tories 1924, helped to defeat General
Strike 1926; Prime Minister 1940-45, 1951-55.

Clemenceau, Georges (1841-1929); French politician, originally
radical but strike-breaker before 1914; Prime Minister 1917-20,
instigated blockade and intervention against Soviet Union.

Denikin, Anton Ivanovich (1872-1947); Tsarist general in World
War I; led counter-revolutionary forces in south during civil war;
defeated at Orel (1919), resigned 1920; lived in exile in France till
1945, then USA.

Dzerzhinsky, Felix (1877-1926); Polish Social Democrat;

imprisoned five times under Tsarism; liberated from ten years
forced labour by February revolution; became prominent
Bolshevik and permanent chair of the Special Commission; died
after attacking opposition at Central Committee meeting.

Glazunov, Alexander (1865-1936); composer of symphonies, etc.,
studied under Rimsky-Korsakov; given title People's Artist of the
Republic; emigrated to Paris 1928.

Gorky, Maxim (1868-1936); pseudonym of A M Peshkov; Russian
novelist and dramatist, author of *Mother* and *The Lower Depths;*
worked with Bolsheviks 1905-17, raised money for them in USA;
critical of repressive measures in early years of Bolshevik rule;
lived abroad 1921-31; in last years made peace with Stalin and
became advocate of 'socialist realism'.

Jaurès, Jean (1859-1914); leader of reformist wing of French
Socialist Party; assassinated on eve of World War I.

Kolchak, Alexander (1873-1920); Tsarist admiral, commanded
Black Sea fleet 1916; established anti-Bolshevik government in
Siberia, proclaimed himself 'supreme ruler' of Russia; Czechs
handed him over to Bolsheviks, who tried and shot him.

Krasin, Leonid (1870-1926); on Bolshevik Central Committee
1903; broke with Lenin 1909, trained as engineer; manager of
Siemens factory in Petrograd; rejoined Bolsheviks 1917, later
ambassador in London and Paris; prestige as engineer helped to
attract technicians to Bolshevik side.

Kropotkin, Pyotr (1842-1921); Russian prince, zoologist,
geographer, historian of the French Revolution and influential
theoretician of anarchism; lived in England 1886-1917; supported
Allies in World War I; returned to Russia 1917, supported
Kerensky, hostile to Bolsheviks.

Lepetit, Jules, Marius (1889-1920); pseudonym of Louis Alexandre
Bertho; French anarchist; worked as navvy from age eleven;
refused to serve in World War I - jailed 1917-19 for publishing
illegal anti-war paper; visited Russia 1920, went to Ukraine;
critical of Bolsheviks, but not hostile; died at sea on return journey
(with Vergeat and Raymond Lefebvre).

Makhno, Nestor (1889-1934); born of peasant family in Ukraine;
became anarchist 1906, imprisoned, released after February 1917;
returned to Ukraine, organised bands of armed peasants, created

anarchist communes, failed to develop urban base; 1919 made alliance with Communists to fight Denikin, but refused to move to Polish front, attacked by Red Army; new alliance with Communists in 1920, but this too broke down; Makhno's forces smashed by Red Army; fled to Paris, died in poverty.

Pestaña, Angel (1881-1937); Spanish anarchist, member of CNT (National Confederation of Labour); later formed syndicalist party; became commissar in Republican Army in Spanish Civil War.

Peters, Iakov Khristoforovich (1886-1938); Latvian Communist from 1904; in London from 1909, member of British Socialist Party; returned to Russia 1917; on Petrograd Military Revolutionary Committee October 1917; deputy chair of Special Commission; 1923 leading figure in GPU; disappeared during purges of 1930s.

Shatov, Bill (Vladimir); Russian anarchist, emigrated to USA, active in Industrial Workers of the World; birth control campaigner; returned to Russia 1917; 1919 officer in Red Army; 1920 Minister of Transport in Far Eastern Republic; later supervised construction of Turkestan-Siberia Railway; 1936, sent to Siberia and probably shot.

Vergeat, Joseph Victor (1891-1920); French syndicalist, active in Syndicalist Youth and as anti-militarist before 1914; campaigned actively against World War I; militant in metal workers' union, secretary of Committee for Third International, 1919; visited Russia 1920; died at sea on return journey (with Lepetit and Raymond Lefebvre).

Voline (1882-1945); pseudonym of Boris Eichenbaum; joined Social Revolutionaries 1904, sentenced to deportation 1907, fled to France; became anarchist 1911; 1915 left France for USA to escape internment for anti-war activity; returned to Russia 1917; editor *Golos Truda*, fought with Makhno in Ukraine; Serge and friends intervened to save his life; left Russia 1922 for Berlin, then Paris.

Yudenich, Nikolay Nikolayevich (1862-1933); Tsarist general; commander-in-chief of counter-revolutionary northwestern army in civil war; after defeat emigrated to Britain.

Zhuk, Iustin Petrovich (1887-1919); from peasant family; expelled from agricultural school for distributing illegal literature; joined anarchists; 1909 sentenced to penal servitude for life for role in 1905 revolution; organised Red Guards in Schlüsselberg after February 1917.

Zinoviev, Grigory (1883-1936); Bolshevik from 1903, worked closely with Lenin; president of Petrograd soviet and President of Communist International 1919-26; allied with Stalin against Trotsky 1923, with Trotsky against Stalin 1925; expelled from Party 1927, capitulated 1928, expelled and readmitted 1932, executed 1936.

ORGANISATIONS

Allies: The alliance in and after World War I led by Britain and France, and including several other states, notably Japan, Italy and the USA.

Cheka: see Special Commission.

Entente: 1907-17 the 'Triple Entente' of France, Britain and Russia; Russia repudiated this after October 1917, and hereafter the term refers to Britain and France.

Jacobins: the most radical bourgeois current in the French revolution, dominant 1793-94; advocated revolutionary terror and an egalitarian republic of small property owners.

Social Revolutionaries: Russian peasant socialist party, formed at the beginning of the century from various Narodnik tendencies; during revolution split: right supported Kerensky; left had anarchistic tendencies, but for a time supported Bolsheviks.

Special Commission: in full Special Commission for the Repression of Counter-Revolution, Speculation, Espionage and Desertion, known as Cheka (from abbreviation of Russian title) established as security force in 1917; replaced by GPU in 1922.

Whites: blanket term for all counter-revolutionary forces during civil war.